An Incomplete Crash Course in Contemporary Music Theory

The Fundamentals

Jeff Bratz

Sign up for the HarmonyTabs email list to keep up with new music releases, upcoming publications, and promotions:

HARMONYTABS EMAIL LIST

(https://www.harmonytabs.com/email-list/)

AN INCOMPLETE CRASH COURSE IN CONTEMPORARY MUSIC THEORY:
THE FUNDAMENTALS

ISBN: 978-1-961735-02-6 (paperback)
ISBN: 978-1-961735-03-3 (ebook)

Library of Congress Control Number: 2023912781

First paperback edition November 2023

Printed in the United States of America

HarmonyTabs Music

HarmonyTabsMusic.com

What's In This Book?

Preface

Why an "incomplete" crash course?

I want to give you enough info to get you up and running without discouraging you. Each of the topics discussed, even in this book of fundamentals, could easily become a book on their own. But what you'll find in these pages is plenty to jumpstart your musical journey.

Why "contemporary" music theory?

The hard and fast rules of classical theory are important to learn, but many of those "rules" are negotiable today. Since most of us live today and not centuries ago, contemporary music theory is probably more useful to you right now.

Anything else I should know?

The next couple pages have a cheat sheet of what you'll learn in this book and a "paper piano". I recommend making copies of these so you can refer to them as you go.

There's a QR code (or a site you can manually enter if you feel so inclined) at the bottom of this page which takes you to audio/video examples found throughout this book. Use them to further your understanding of the concepts.

I think you now know everything you need to get going!

Audio/Video Examples

(harmonytabs.com/the-fundamentals/)

An Incomplete Crash Course In Contemporary Music Theory: The Fundamentals

Cheat Sheet

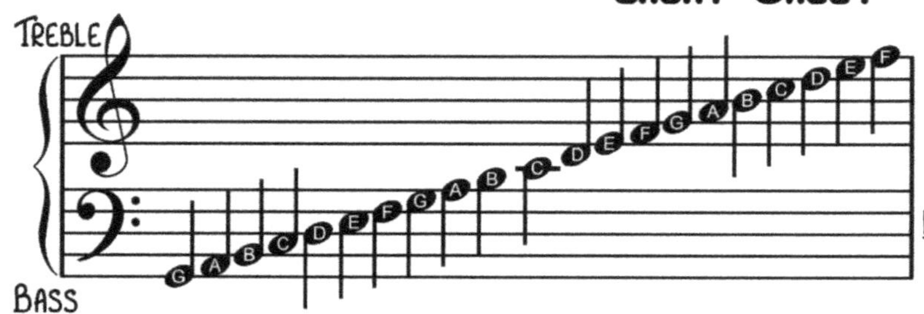

TREBLE
LINES = Every Good Boy Does Fine
SPACES = FACE on space

BASS
LINES = Good Boys Deserve Fudge Always
SPACES = All Cows Eat Grass

Time Signatures

4 = Beats Per Measure

4 = What Gets The Beat

Simple	Compound	Irregular
2 3 4 2	6 9 12	5 7
4 4 4 2	8 8 8	4 4

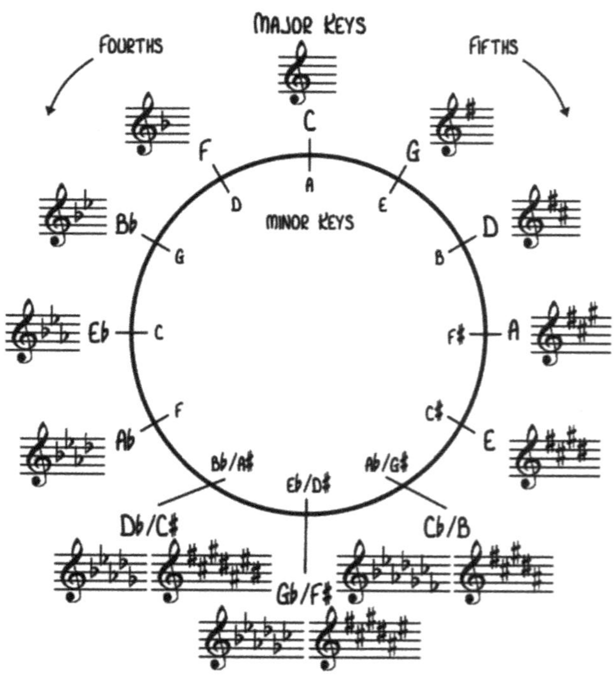

Accidentals

♭ = Flat
♮ = Natural
♯ = Sharp

The Circle of Fifths

Dots Add Additional 1/2 Duration

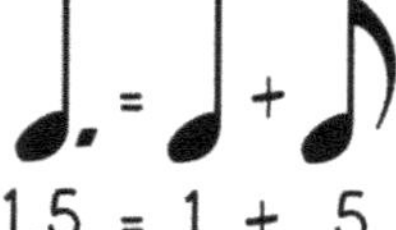
1.5 = 1 + .5

MAJOR SCALE STEPS = Whole-Whole-Half W-W-W-H
MINOR SCALE STEPS = W-H W-W-H W-W

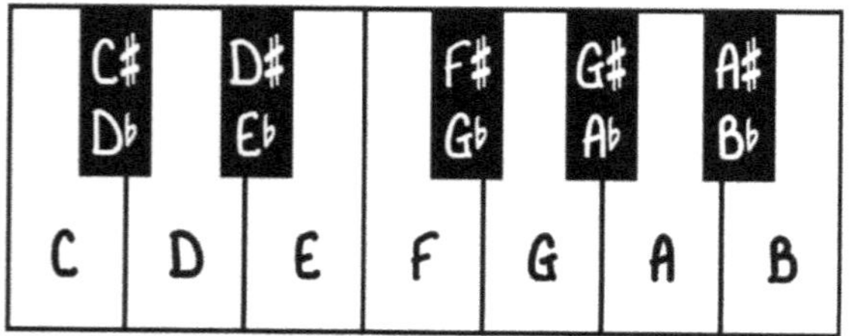

Line of Fourths (flat keys) = B E A D G C F Bb Eb Ab Db Gb

Line of Fifths (sharp keys) = F C G D A E B

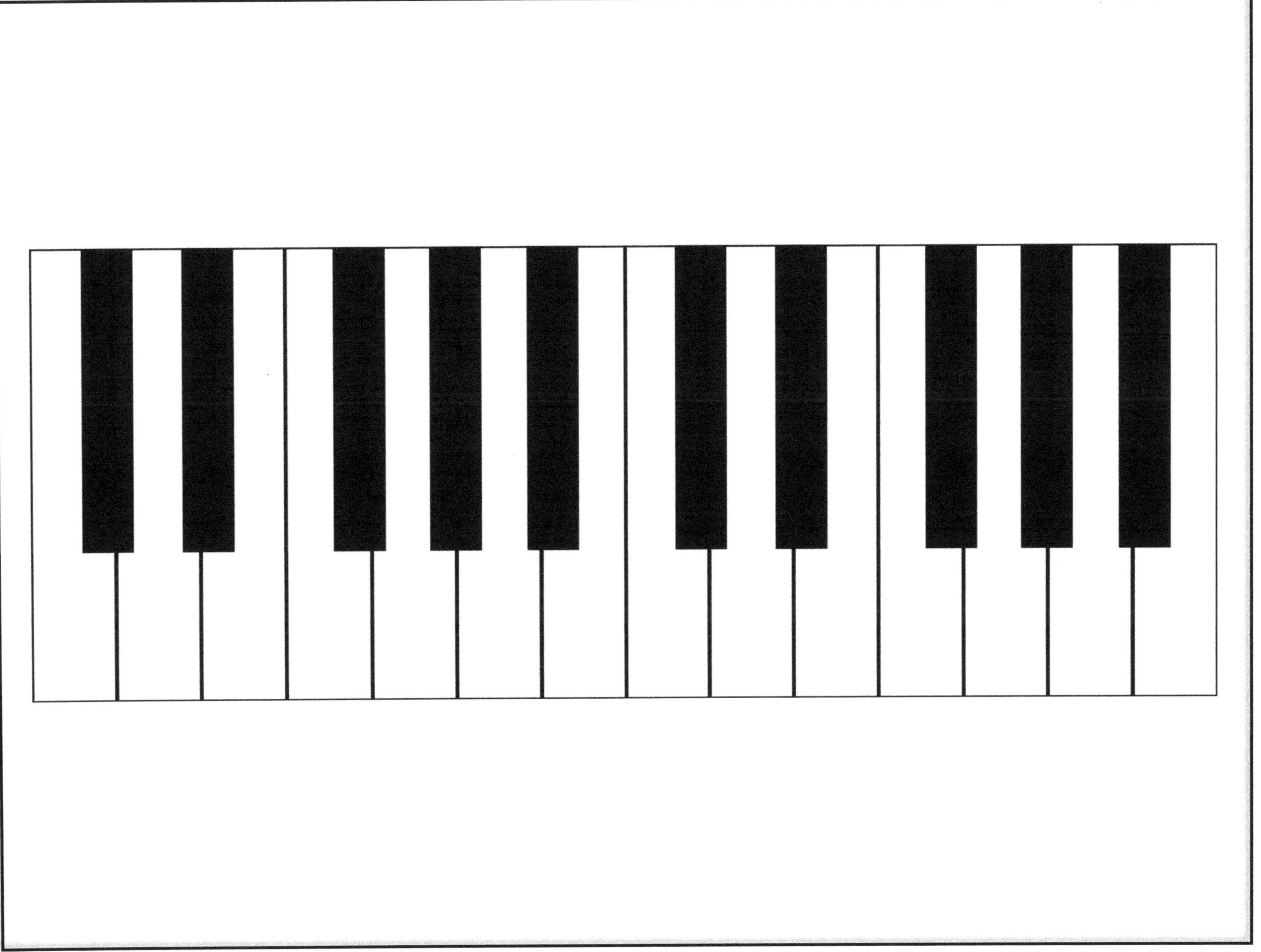

Copy this page or rip it out so you can use it as you go through this book!

INTRO

"Jeff. You're never going to be good. You'll only ever be just better than bad."

This is what P.M., the guy that ran my music school, said to me shortly before he dropped me from the top vocal jazz group on campus. I like to imagine there was some philosophical lesson to be learned from these inspired words, but I have yet to figure them out.

When I showed up to music school, I was pretty sure I was gonna breeze through… because I was top of my singing game back in high school. It started out that way when I secured a spot in the coveted I.V. run by P.M. himself. I got ousted about a month into school and dropped down to another group.

I didn't lose my spot because I couldn't sing the material. I lost my spot because I didn't understand theory, how the chords worked, or which notes I was supposed to be painstakingly plunking out at the piano. I couldn't keep up!

That's when I realized I really needed to level-up if I was ever going to be a professional musician. So, I did!

But it didn't happen overnight. I started by learning what the notes on the page are and how they all fit together to create music. That's where everyone has to start. The fundamentals.

By the time you make it through this book, you'll probably have more questions than answers. And that's good! That'll drive your musical journey. But you'll also have a solid foundation to stand on when you move forward.

You'll know what you're looking at on that sheet of music from the rhythms notated, to the notes to be played, to the key of the tune; and how they all work together in "harmony".

The entire purpose of this book is to take the mystery out of the musical language. All those dots and lines and scribbles on a page of music can look daunting, but they don't have to! And I want to help you get over that music-phobia.

So, grab a pencil and some staff paper and dive into one of the most fulfilling learning experiences a person can embark on!

-Jeff

CHAPTER 1
STAFF BASICS

Let's begin with the basic of the basics… the **staff**. This is the set of horizontal lines music is generally written on. This is also where the majority of all your music-ing is going to happen. But the staff is much more useful with a few additions.

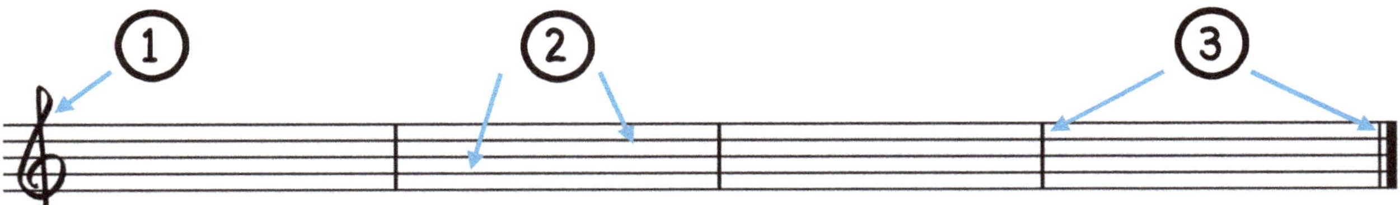

1 – The Clef

You'll run into a number of squiggly symbols on the far left of the staff. These tell you what the notes on the staff are.

2 – Lines and Spaces

On each staff, regardless of the clef, there will be five lines and four spaces. This is where the music notes go.

3 – Bar Lines

Bar lines serve a number of purposes. The only thing you need to know right now is that they separate the staff into bars or measures. The image above shows four measures.

THE CRASH

-The **staff** has a **clef**, **five lines** and **four spaces**, and **bar lines**

Let's put our staff knowledge to use.

CHAPTER 2
RHYTHM AND THE BEAT

Before we get too deep into the notes themselves, we need to talk about **rhythm**. Rhythm is one of the foundational elements of music. It's what makes you tap your foot to your favorite tune. Without it we just have a slew of notes that don't know what they're doing.

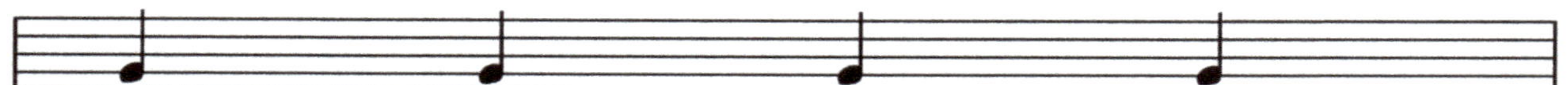

Four is the magic number when it comes to most Western music. *Western music* just means it comes from a European background, and most of what you listen to probably does. Much of that music is in 4/4 time. Four beats per measure and the quarter note marks the beat, like in the image above. We'll dive into time signatures and what 4/4 means in a bit. For now, just know there are four quarter notes in a measure.

But what's a quarter note?

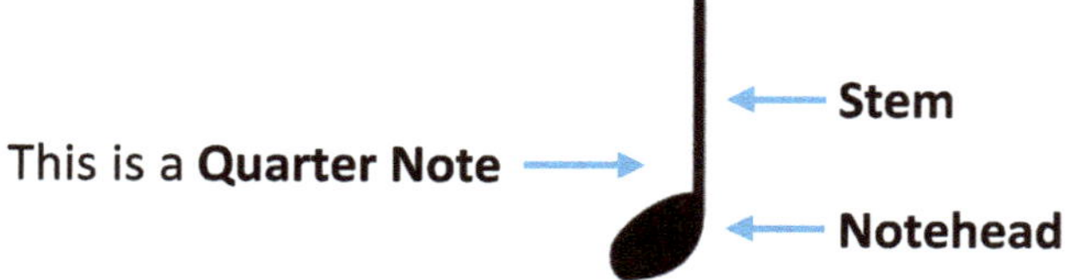

A quarter note has a **filled-in notehead** with a line coming off the side called the **stem**. It kinda looks like a golf club. This guy is the workhorse for a lot of music.

THE CRASH

-The **quarter note** gets the beat... for now

Let's look at some other notes.

CHAPTER 3
NOTES AND DURATIONS

If we only worked with quarter notes, the tunes would be pretty boring. So, let's add some others. Here are the main notes and their **durations**, or length of each note, you'll work with.

Whole Note = = 4 beats

The whole note is just a hollow oval.

Half Note = = 2 beats

The half note looks like a hollow quarter note.

Quarter Note = = 1 beat

We've already seen the quarter note.

Eighth Note = = 1/2 beat

The eighth note looks like a quarter note with a *single flag*.

Sixteenth Note = = 1/4 beat

The sixteenth note looks like a quarter note with a *double flag*.

If the quarter note gets the beat, why is it called a "quarter" note?

Time signatures will help, which we'll get into a little later. For now, the simple explanation is that a *whole note fills one measure* and the rest of the notes are based on their relationship to the whole note.

Or to put it another way…

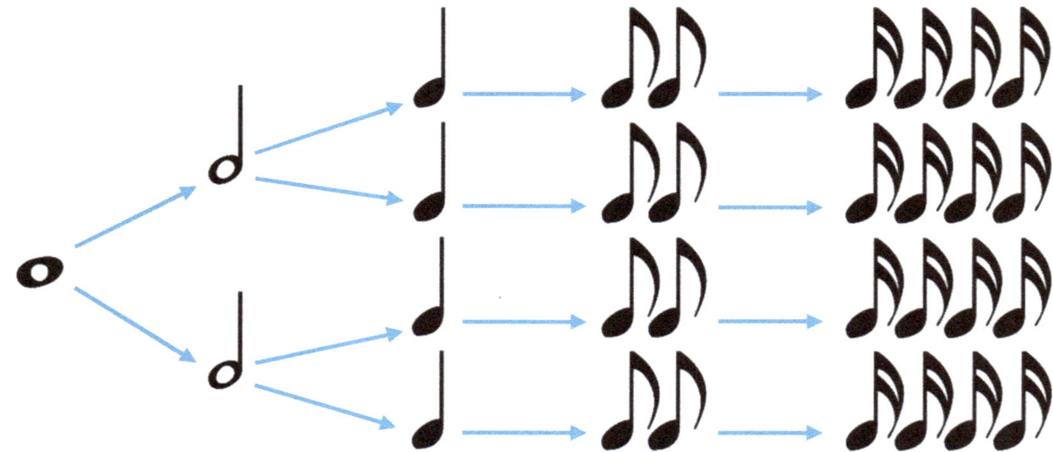

1 whole note = 2 half notes = 4 quarter notes = 8 eighth notes = 16 sixteenth notes.

It's pretty easy to see that working with eighth notes and sixteenth notes could get unruly in a quick hurry if written as individual notes like above.

That brings us to the wonderful world of beaming!

BEAMING

Beaming connects those smaller notes, eighth notes and sixteenth notes, in a sensical way to make them easier to read. And it's exactly as it sounds… you beam the single notes together.

<u>Instead of this...</u>   <u>...you get this.</u>

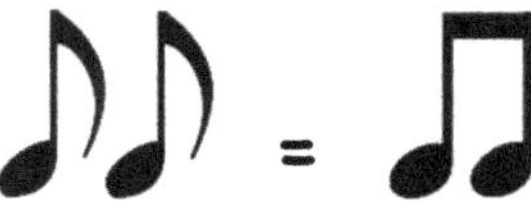

2 eighth notes get beamed together with a single beam. **1 flag, 1 beam**.

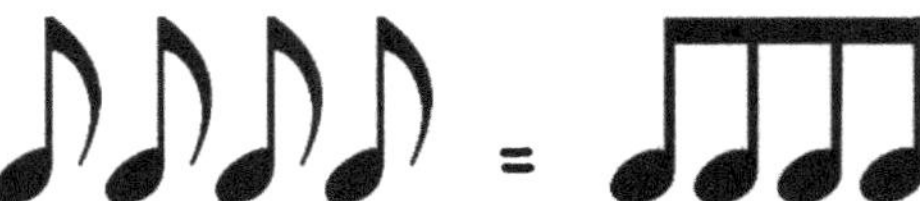

4 eighth notes also get beamed together. 4 is also a magic number when it comes to beaming. Keeping beams to 4 and under makes the music much more legible. 4 eighth notes beamed together is equal to 1 half note, or 2 quarter notes.

2 sixteenth notes get beamed together with a double beam. **2 flags, 2 beams**.

4 sixteenth notes also get beamed together. Again, top out your beaming at 4 notes. 4 sixteenth notes beamed together is equal to 1 quarter note.

So now instead of this...

...you get this.

Much cleaner and easier to read!

Neat. I now know what all these notes look like, and you've told me about their duration, but how do I actually put that into practice??

Now it starts to get fun!

COUNTING

With all these rhythms in hand, counting lets you accurately perform them for the world.

We've already decided we're working with 4 beats in a measure (for now) and the quarter note equals 1 beat.

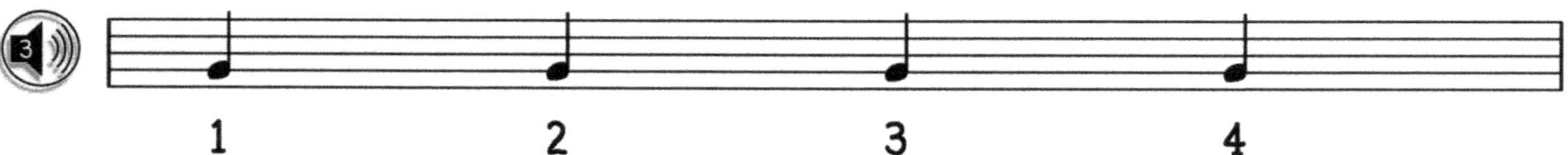

1 **2** **3** **4**

That was a pretty easy start. *4 notes, 4 beats*. The math does itself. These 4 beats are the foundation for all the rest of the counting.

> ***Quick Note!*** **The Beat**
>
> It's important to understand that the beat is *consistent and even*. No matter what we get into for the rest of counting, you should be able to evenly clap 1, 2, 3, 4. Everything else fills in around that even beat.

Let's look at the rest of the notes, starting with the whole note.

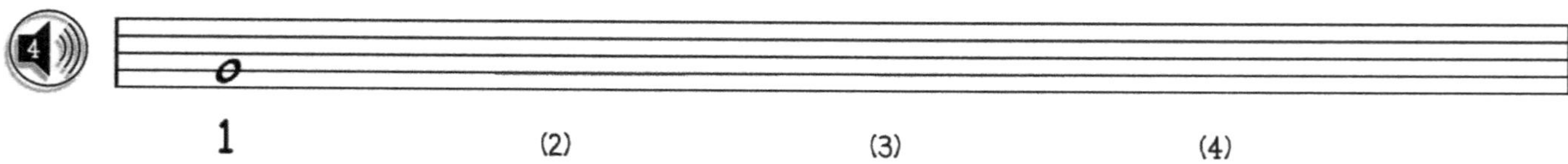

1 (2) (3) (4)

The whole note starts on beat 1 and is **sustained** (or continuously sounded) for **4 beats**. Beats 2, 3, and 4 still exist, but they aren't restruck (or replayed). We'll put the beats that aren't restruck in parentheses just so you can see where they are.

Like the whole note, the half note has some ghosted beats in it. The half note is sustained for **2 beats**, but the second beat isn't restruck. With 2 half notes, the first one takes up beats 1 and 2 and the second takes up beats 3 and 4.

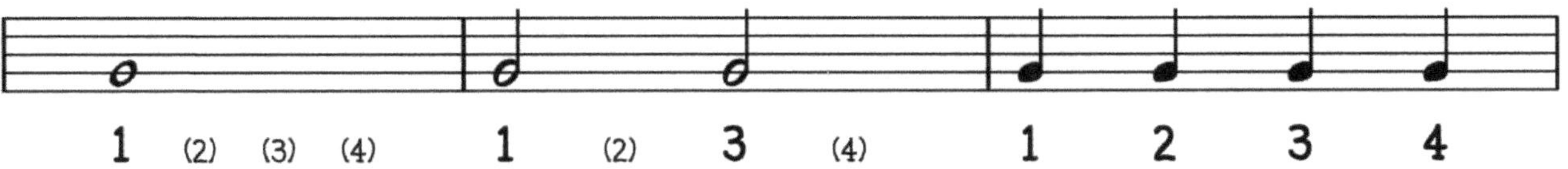

We've already talked about the quarter note taking **1 beat**. **1, 2, 3, 4**.

The eighth note is where things start to get interesting. An eighth note gets **1/2 beat**. It has all the beats of the quarter note, but also has beats in-between. You count these as "**&**" ("*and*"). You still have the **1, 2, 3,** and **4** (the **on-beats**) in the same place as the quarter notes, but the "**&**"s land on the **off-beats**. Giving us **1 & 2 & 3 & 4 &**.

Sixteenth notes have twice as many beats as eighth notes. Each one is **1/4 beat**. We have to add "**e**" ("*ee*") and "**a**" ("*uh*") to the mix, giving us "**1 e & a**" ("*one ee and uh*"). So, the on-beats from the quarter notes and the off-beats from the eighth notes still land in the same place; now there are a couple extras added in.

And these notes can all be mixed in together.

If you can get this concept, **counting**, you can read the rhythms of nearly any piece of music you run into!

But, of course, there are a couple things that complicate this clear-cut system.

TIES AND DOTS

Ties and dots add more functionality to notes. They allow you to extend the duration of notes so you're not stuck with just the standard note lengths.

Ties

Let's first deal with ties. A **tie** *ties* multiple notes together to form a longer note. This is generally used to cross bar lines into another measure or to cross the *imaginary bar line*… which we'll discuss in a bit.

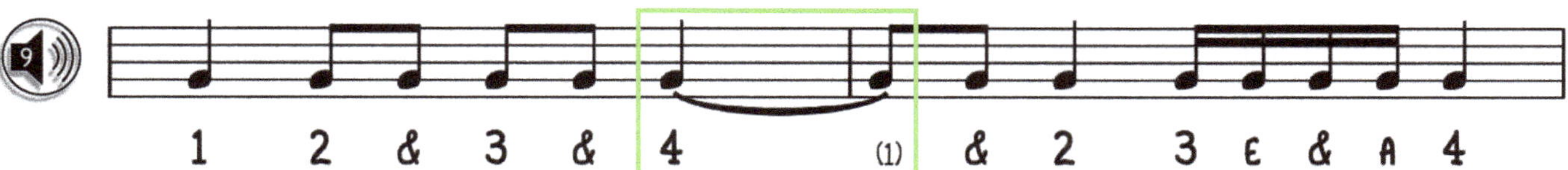

You can never cross a bar line with a note. It would just make a mess of the music. Instead, you can toss a tie in there and it's *like* crossing a bar line.

In the above example we've tied beat 4 of the first measure to the first half of beat 1 of the second measure. Now instead of the quarter note on beat 4 being worth 1 beat, it combines with the eighth note to become 1.5 beats... 1 beat + .5 beats.

You can do this with any note duration and across as many measures as you want.

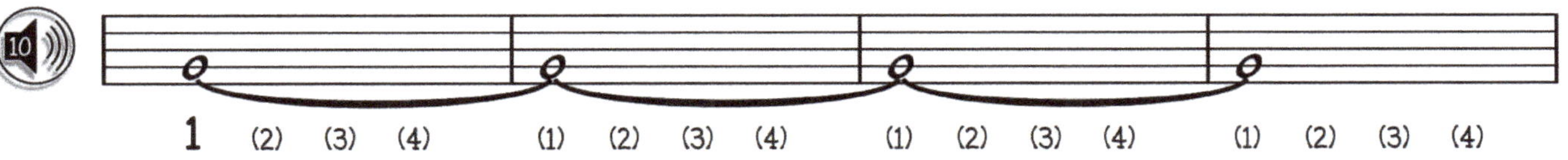

A single whole note is 4 beats. 4 whole notes tied together becomes 16 beats.

You can see how this opens up a whole slew of new possibilities.

Dots

The other operator that adds more duration to a note is the **Dot**. This one is more specific. While you can use a tie to tie *any* two notes together to create *any* new duration, the dot only adds an **additional half duration** to whichever note you put it after.

𝅗𝅥. = 𝅝 + 𝅗𝅥 = 6 BEATS
4 + 2

𝅗𝅥. = 𝅗𝅥 + 𝅘𝅥 = 3 BEATS
2 + 1

𝅘𝅥. = 𝅘𝅥 + 𝅘𝅥𝅮 = 1.5 BEATS
1 + .5

𝅘𝅥𝅮. = 𝅘𝅥𝅮 + 𝅘𝅥𝅯 = .75 BEATS
.5 + .25

A couple things to notice:

When you get down to eighth notes and sixteenth notes, dots can get tricky.

And you'll notice I didn't use a dotted whole note in the example. *Why?* Because we're working with a 4 beat measure. A dotted whole note is 6 beats and we're *not allowed to cross the bar line* into the next measure. You'd need a bar with 6 beats to have a dotted whole note.

THE CRASH

NOTES AND DURATION

-A measure can have:

**1 whole note, 2 half notes, 4 quarter notes,
8 eighth notes, or 16 sixteenth notes**
Or,
**1 whole note = 2 half notes = 4 quarter notes
= 8 eighth notes = 16 sixteenth notes**

BEAMING

-**Beaming** really cleans up the music, making it easier to read
-**Eighth notes** get a **single beam,** and
-**Sixteenth notes** get a **double beam**
-Both can be beamed in groups of **2 or 4**

COUNTING

-**Counting** is the key to nailing rhythms
-The **beat** is **consistent and even**

With 4 beats in a measure...

-The **whole note** gets struck on beat 1 and is sustained for
4 beats
-The **half note** is sustained for **2 beats**
-The **quarter note** gets **1 beat**
-The **eighth note** is **1/2 beat**
-The **sixteenth note** is **1/4 beat**

TIES AND DOTS

-**Ties** and **dots** add duration to notes.
-Ties combine notes, often over bar lines, to extend the
duration
-A dot adds an extra half to the duration of the note it
follows

I want to touch on one more rhythmic idea that you'll encounter pretty frequently.

CHAPTER 4
TUPLETS

Tuplets create a subdivision of a rhythm that wouldn't normally be found in the music. This can add an additional "surprise" factor to the music - or just create a different groove in your tune than what might be expected.

TRIPLET

The most common tuplet is the triplet. It takes a rhythm of *2 beats* and turns it into *3 beats* of the same length.

This, again, is your standard 4 quarter note bar.

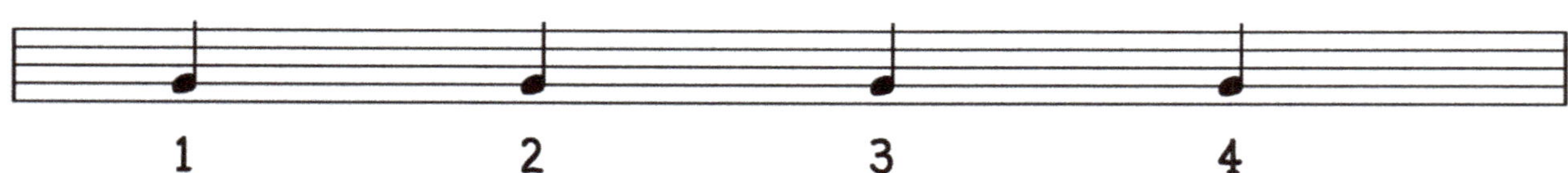

If we turn the last 2 quarter notes into a triplet it becomes...

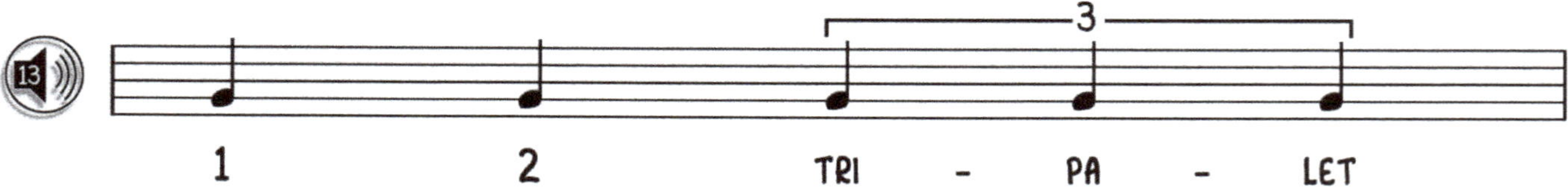

To see how these rhythms line up against each other, let's put them on the same staff.

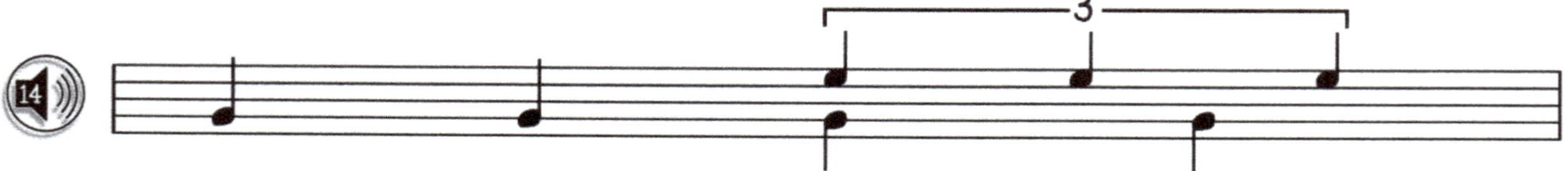

Notice that the first note of the triplet lines up with the regular quarter note. The second quarter note falls between the last 2 notes of the triplet. In the same way that the 2 regular quarter notes are rhythmically even when you count them, the 3 notes of the triplet are evenly spaced to take up the same length as the 2 regular quarter notes.

Triplets can be used with any type of note.

Here's a set of standard eighth notes on beats "4 &".

Here's that set of eighth notes turned into a triplet.

And here they are on the same staff.

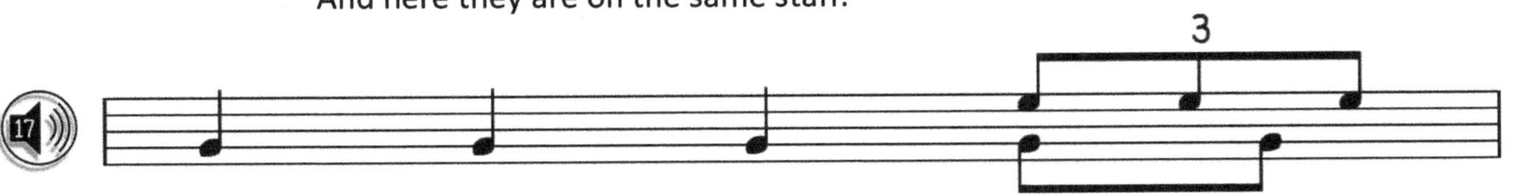

You can go even further with sixteenth notes and beyond if you want/need to; or go larger, for that matter, with half notes and beyond. The same concepts apply with other note types.

Quarter notes and eighth notes are the most common triplet divisions.

OTHER TUPLETS

You can divide notes into many different tuplets. For the sake of simplicity, and since you aren't likely to see many other than triplets, I'm not going to go too far into those here. Below are a couple examples.

As with triplets, other tuplets need to take up the same duration as the notes that *would* be there. In the examples above, the quintuplet and septuplet both need to take up the space of 2 quarter notes.

If you don't like "Opp-or-tu-ni-ty" or "In-com-pa-ti-bi-li-ty" feel free to come up with any 5 or 7 syllable words to help you keep time!

THE CRASH

-**Tuplets** can be a fun way to add interest to a rhythm

-**Triplets** are the most common tuplet you'll run into

There's one more important concept to understand with regard to making the music easier to read.

CHAPTER 5
THE IMAGINARY BAR LINE

It sounds fake, and in a way it is. The imaginary bar line divides the measure so each of the beats is easier to read. In general, if you have a measure with 4 beats, you need to be able to clearly see beats 1 and 3.

Which makes it easier to find all 4 beats?

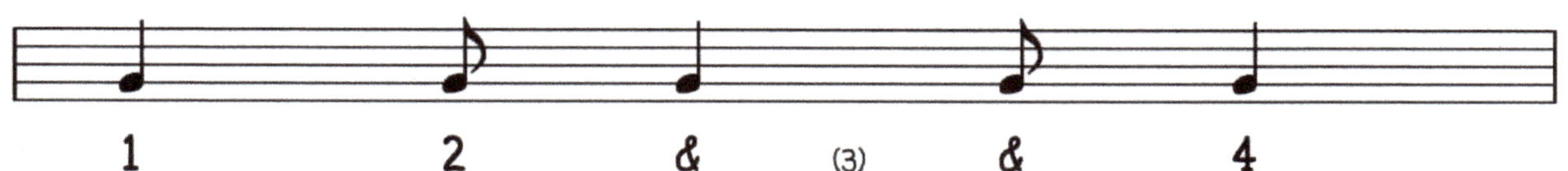

or

I'm hoping for the sake of my point you chose the second example. Both show the same rhythm, but notice how beat 3 in the second example is clearly shown, even if it isn't *struck* on 3. This small detail becomes a huge detail when trying to read a piece of music.

The Imaginary Bar Line!

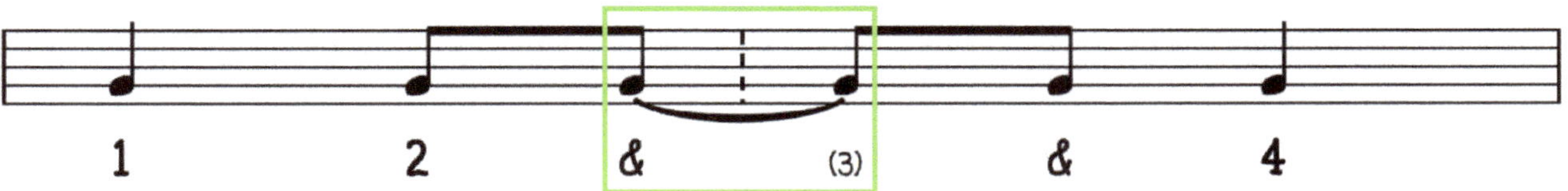

Staying in 4/4 time (4 quarter notes and the quarter note gets the beat), the imaginary bar line lands between beats 2 and 3. It's never actually *shown* as a line (or dotted line as above) in a piece of music, but it's always *implied* when writing music.

Instead of placing a quarter note on the "&" of 2, you tie 2 eighth notes (each worth 1/2 beat, totaling 1 beat) together across the imaginary bar line.

Of course, there are "rules" and exceptions.

First, the generally accepted exceptions to the rule.

Generally Accepted Exceptions

Whole Notes

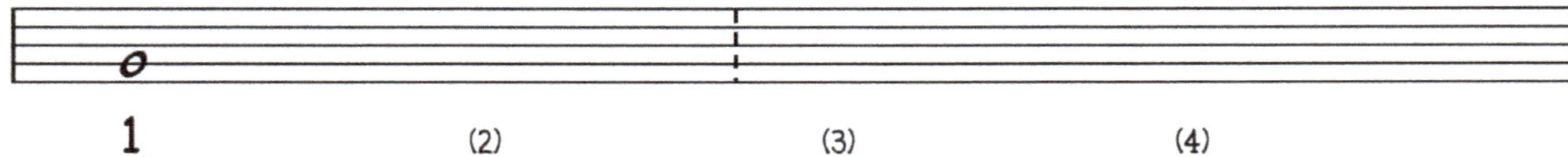

Whole notes can cross the Imaginary Bar Line to take up a whole measure. It'd be silly if they couldn't. A whole note is 4 beats, a measure is 4 beats.

(*Some*) Half Notes

Half notes are long enough, 2 beats, that crossing the imaginary bar line is okay… when it lands on an *on-beat* but *not an off-beat*. It doesn't confuse things too much.

Same goes for a dotted half note. Duration of 3 beats doesn't confuse things when placed on an *on-beat*.

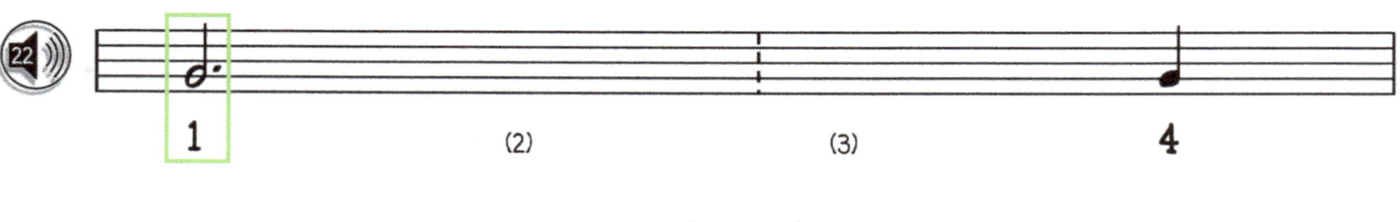

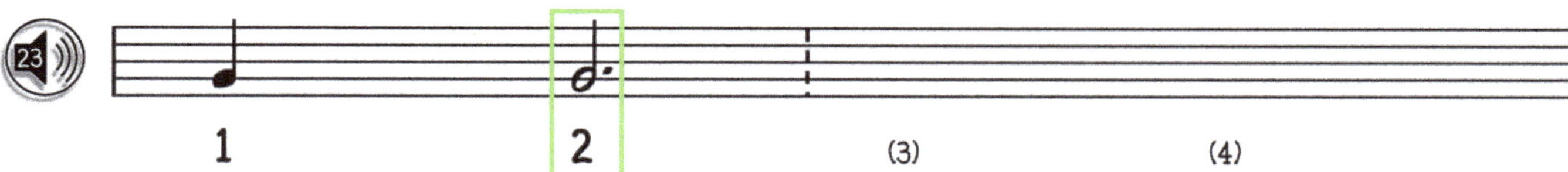

However…

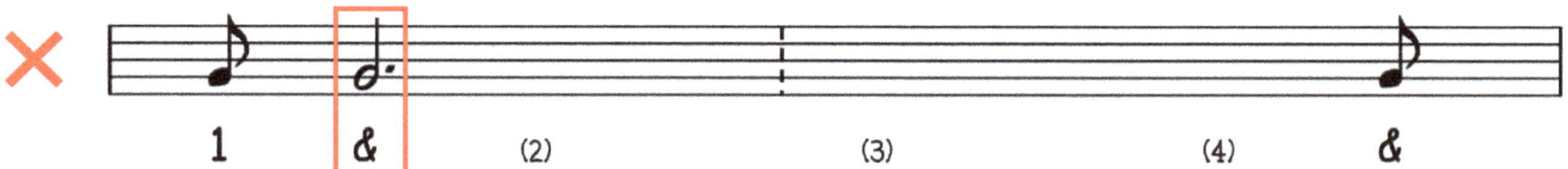

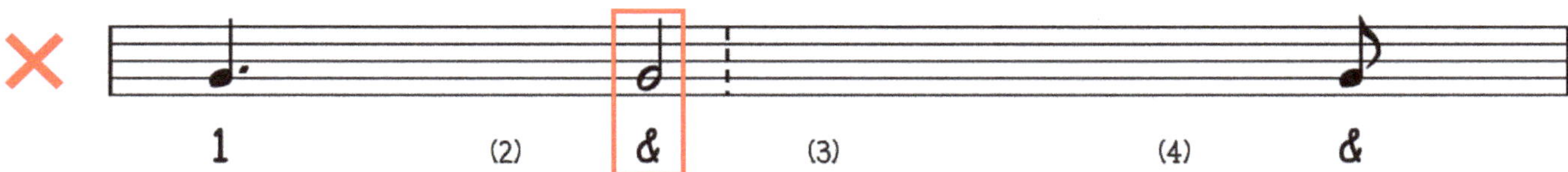

…starting a half note or dotted half note on an *off-beat* makes the notation pretty ugly and hard to read. Stick to putting them on the on-beats and you'll be okay.

Now the generally followed rules.

Generally Followed Rules

Quarter Notes

We saw this one earlier. Quarter notes should (*almost always*) land on the *on-beat*. To fix this, we tie a couple eighth notes together over the imaginary bar line. A quarter note is 1 beat, 2 eighth notes is 1 beat.

There is one **generally accepted exception** to this: *3 quarter notes in a row* which start on the *off-beat* of 1, or the "&" of 1.

This has become such a common **syncopated rhythm** (**syncopation**: *placing strong beats on the off-beats*) that you'll often see it written as above. But it's also perfectly acceptable to write it like this...

Eighth Notes

Eighth notes follow the same basic principle as quarter notes... show beats 1 and 3. However, you have some options.

and

are both perfectly acceptable. You can either beam in groups of 2 starting on the on-beat to form full single beats, like the first example above, or in groups of 4 starting on the on-beat to form 2 full beats like the second example. Sometimes one option is better than the other, depending on what you're trying to do. Choose your own adventure!

Don't start your eighth note beam groups on off-beats.

You can see that the on-beats aren't clearly defined above. That makes reading it tough.

Sixteenth Notes

The shorter the note duration, the smaller the beam groups. Also, you need to be more precise with the beaming since music gets harder to read with shorter notes.

When you get down to sixteenth notes, you add a couple extra imaginary bar lines to separate out all 4 beats.

If using 2 sixteenth notes where an eighth note would go…

or

…they need to start where the eighth note would have started. So, either on the on-beat ("1") or on the off-beat ("&"). In this case, the sixteenth notes beam directly to the eighth note to complete the beat.

This doesn't apply when there are just eighth notes. The eighth notes on beats "3 & 4 &" can beam in a group of 4 across this new imaginary bar line.

Don't start a double sixteenth note on the "e" or the "a".

The two examples above are both really ugly to read because they don't start *where an eighth note would have started*.

4 sixteenth notes beamed together should start and complete a single beat. They can start on beats 1, 2, 3, or 4… *and nowhere else.*

When 4 sixteenth notes beamed together start anywhere but 1, 2, 3, or 4 you completely lose where the on-beats are supposed to be. No good. Remember, most of these "rules" are in place to make reading the music easier.

THE CRASH

-The **imaginary bar line** splits up a measure to make the music easier to read

-You should (*almost*) always be able to **clearly see the on-beats**

-Generally, you should start quarter notes, groups of eighth notes, and groups of 4 sixteenth notes on the **on-beat**

-Don't start half notes on an off-beat

We've got the notes.

Now let's look at what happens between *the notes.*

CHAPTER 6
RESTS

Rests are exactly as they sound (or *don't* "sound", I suppose); they give the notes a rest from constantly being played (that would make for pretty uninteresting music). In the same way that a note indicates *sound*, a rest indicates *silence*.

Rests have direct durational counterparts to notes.

Whole Rest = = 4 beats

The whole rest is like an upside-down hat.
As though you could fill the *"whole"* hat.

Half Rest = = 2 beats

The half rest looks like a right-side-up hat.

Quarter Rest = = 1 beat

The quarter rest looks a bit like a lightning bolt.

Eighth Rest = = 1/2 beat

The eighth rest sort of resembles a fancy "7".

Sixteenth Rest =   = 1/4 beat

And the sixteenth rest looks like an eighth rest with an extra flag.

To show the associations…

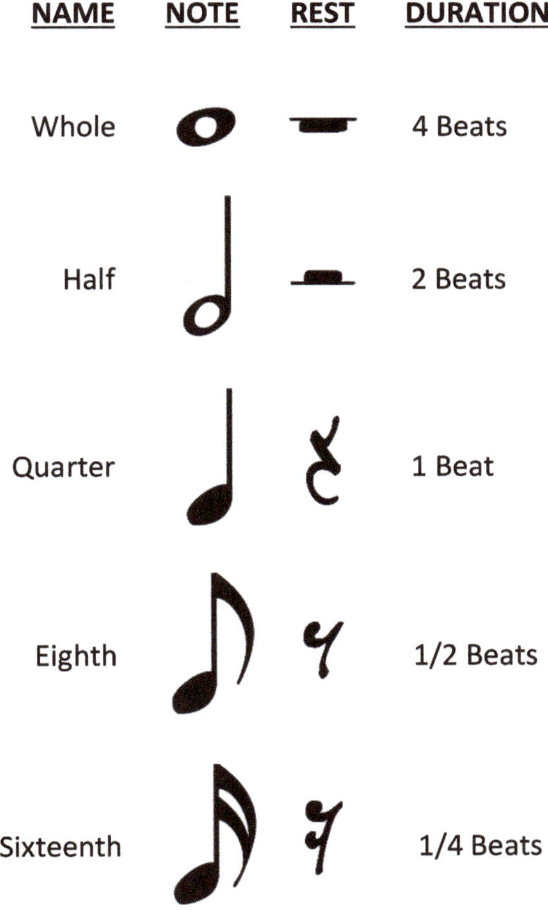

NAME	NOTE	REST	DURATION
Whole			4 Beats
Half			2 Beats
Quarter			1 Beat
Eighth			1/2 Beats
Sixteenth			1/4 Beats

These rests have the same duration as their note counterparts, so they take up the same space.

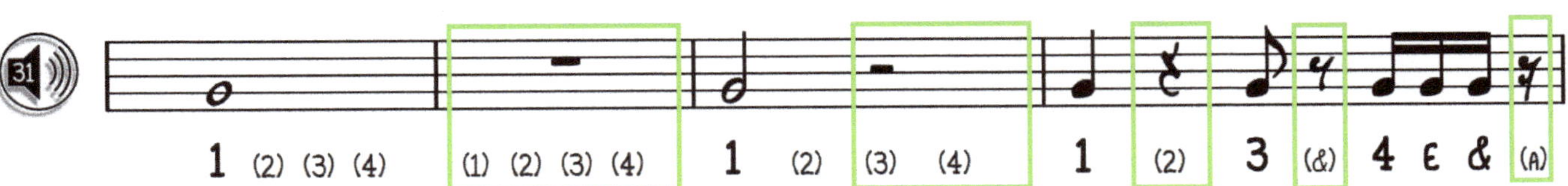

Generally, you can combine smaller rests into a larger rest if you need; but keep in mind that the *imaginary bar line rules apply to rests as well*!

Ties and Dots

Ties – There's never a need to tie rests together since they aren't being sustained.

Dots – You'll occasionally see people use dots to extend rests an extra 1/2 the duration, especially with larger (quarter, half, whole) rests. I don't think it usually cleans anything up and can certainly make things harder to read. But, really, dealer's choice.

REST PLACEMENT

Whole Rest

You can't technically see the horizontal line on top of the whole rest because it's just part of the staff line, but the whole rest goes directly **under the 4ᵗʰ line** from the bottom (or *in* the 3ʳᵈ space from the bottom) and in the **middle of the 4 beats** it takes up.

Half Rest

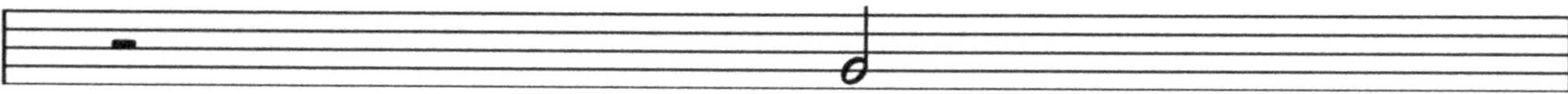

Again, you can't see the horizontal line. The half rest goes directly **above the 3ʳᵈ line** from the bottom (or, again, *in* the 3ʳᵈ space from the bottom) and **at the position the rest starts**. So, as above, if you have a half rest on beats 1 and 2 you should place the half rest at beat 1.

Quarter Rest

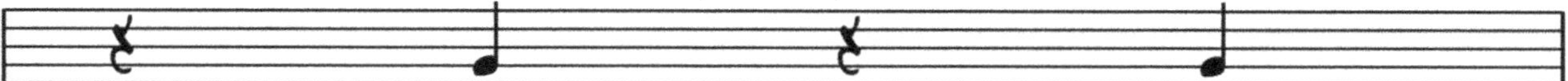

The quarter rest is **centered around the middle of the staff** and **spans just beyond the middle 3 lines**. It should also be **placed at the beat** you want to rest.

Eighth Rest

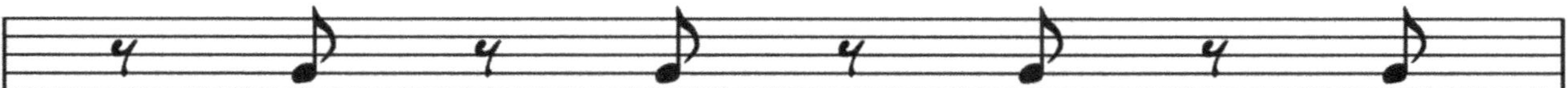

Eighth rests are also **centered around the middle of the staff** and **take up the 2 middle spaces**. You can also think of the **flag resting on top of the 3rd line** from the bottom.

Sixteenth Rest

Sixteenth rests **aren't centered**, but instead have the **top flag resting on the 3rd line** from the bottom and extend basically to the bottom of the staff.

Now, About Rest Placement

One final note on rest placement... everything I just told you may not always work for you. Sometimes the rests just have to go where they have to go. For instance, if you're writing for multiple parts that don't rest at the same time...

...you have to place the rests where they're easiest to read for each part.

THE CRASH

-**Rests** give the music some space to breathe

-For every note value there's an equal rest value to go with it

-Ties and dots are unnecessary with rests

-There are pretty good general placement guidelines for rests that simply don't always cut it

Remember that 4/4 time signature business?

It's time to explain what all that means!

CHAPTER 7
TIME SIGNATURES

Up to this point we've been talking about *4 quarter* notes filling up the *4 beats* of a measure. That's 4/4 time (or *Common Time*). But how did we know that and what are some other options? This is where **time signatures** come in.

This is a time signature. This is the time signature we've been using for all the previous chapters. **4/4**. It's comprised of 2 numbers, one on top of the other. There are time signatures which are more than just the 2 numbers, but they're rare and we're not going to get into those in this book.

So, what do these numbers mean?

4   **Top Number** – *How many beats per measure*

4   **Bottom Number** – *Which note value gets the beat*

Let's dig deeper, starting with the bottom number.

Why start with the bottom number?

It gives you the baseline for what to do with the top number. I'll show you.

Bottom Number

Which note value gets the beat.

In the example above we have a *4*. A 4 indicates that the *quarter note* gets the beat, since in 4/4 time there are *4 quarter notes* in the measure. This basic formula can be used across the board. If the bottom number is a *2*, the *half note* gets the beat... *2 half notes* in a 4/4 bar. If the bottom number is *8*, the *eighth note* gets the beat... *8 eighth notes* in a 4/4 bar.

Top Number

How many beats per measure.

This one's easy. If the top number is 4, there are 4 beats per measure. If the top number is 3, there are 3 beats per measure.

Let's put them together.

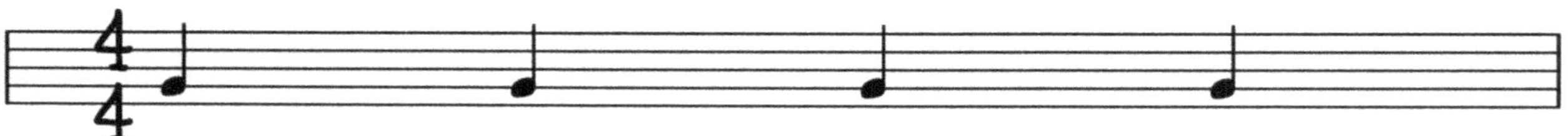

Here we're back to our old friend 4/4.

Bottom number = **4** = *quarter note* gets the beat.

Top number = **4** = 4 beats per measure.

Therefore, there are **4 quarter notes in each measure**.

Let's try another.

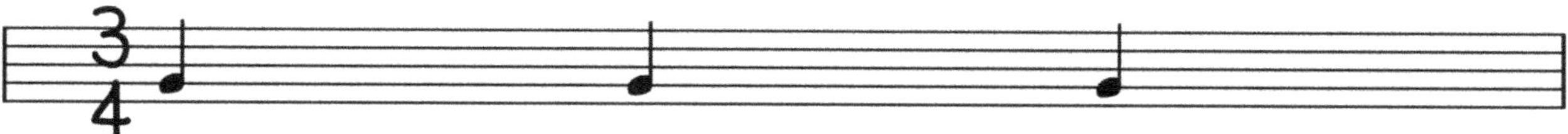

This time signature is 3/4.

Bottom number = **4** = *quarter note* gets the beat.

Top number = **3** = 3 beats per measure.

3 quarter notes in each measure.

Let's go a little crazy this time.

This time signature is 7/8.

Bottom number = **8** = *eighth note* gets the beat.

Top number = **7** = 7 beats per measure.

7 eighth notes in each measure.

Now that you've got the formula for dissecting the time signature, let's talk more in depth about some of the most common time signatures.

Simple Time

Simple time describes a time signature where the top number is a 2, 3, or 4 and has *1 group of beats per measure...* meaning the stressed beat, or *emphasized beat*, is beat 1, or the **downbeat.**

4/4 (aka Common Time)

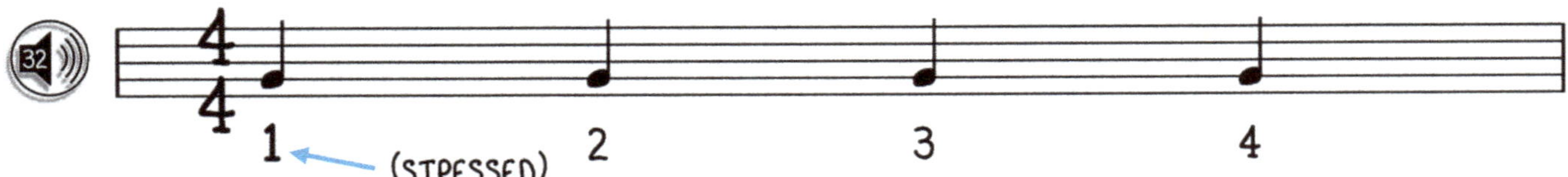

We've already talked a bit about 4/4 time. 4 quarter notes in a bar. The stress is on beat 1. So, you'd count it "**One**-two-three-four".

This is by far the most common time signature you'll encounter. That's why it's also called **Common Time**. You might see it written as a "C" like this…

But you may also not see any time signature at all. That means you're in 4/4.

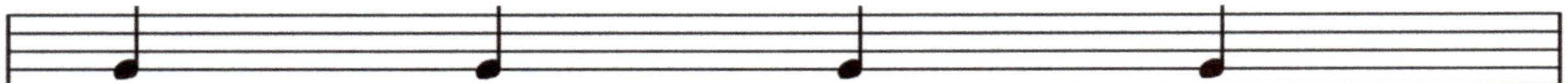

3/4

3/4 time is also very common, but not quite as common as 4/4. Sorry 3/4! 3/4 time gives the music a bit of a lilt, like in a waltz. 3/4 time is counted "**One**-two-three".

2/2 (aka Cut Time)

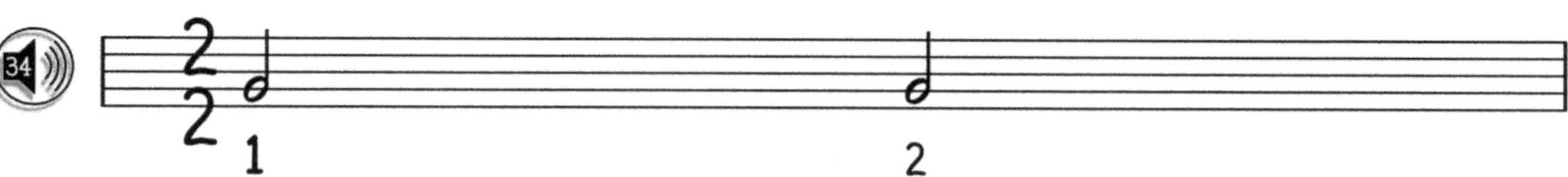

2/2 time seems a little confusing.

Isn't this just 4/4?

Yes, and no. It's basically 4/4 time, but for much faster music like marches. Counting in 2 just makes it a bit easier to keep up. Counted "**One**-two".

Since it is basically 4/4 but counted with the *beats cut in half*, it's more commonly referred to as **cut time** and written as a "C" with a line down the middle, a bit like the symbol for "cents".

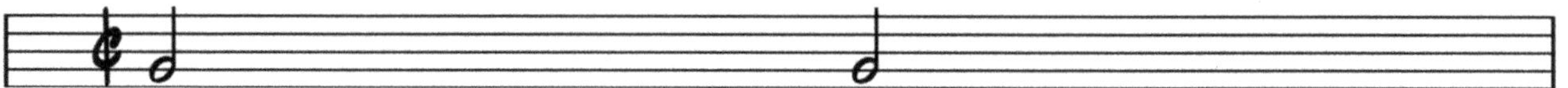

2/4

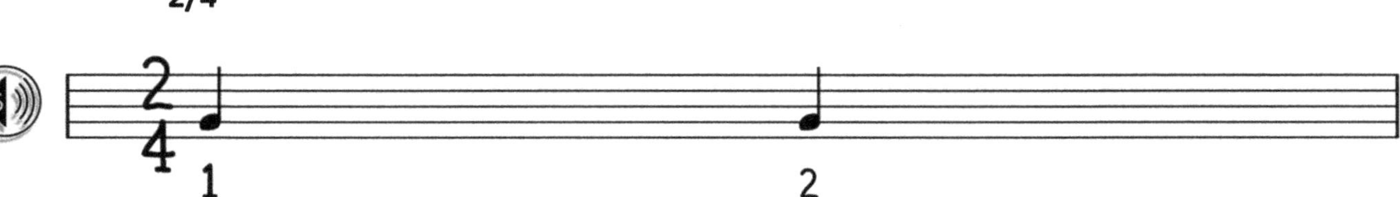

2/4? Okay, now you're messing with me, right?

Afraid not. Seems like you wouldn't really need cut time and 2/4, but there is a difference that makes it worth it. Cut time is usually played pretty fast, whereas 2/4 doesn't need to be. So, the "**One**-two" gives us the "**Oom**-pa" feel of polkas.

COMPOUND TIME

Compound time is bit trickier. It's essentially any time signature where the *top number is a multiple of 3*. Most often you'll find an 8 on the bottom. The notes are usually *grouped into sets of 3* and the first of each of those sets gets the stress.

Sounds a bit confusing. Some examples will help.

6/8

In 6/8 time, the eighth note gets the beat and you have 6 (a multiple of 3) of them. There are 2 sets of 3 eighth notes and the stress happens on the first of each of those sets.

Compound time signatures usually give a lilt similar to what you find in 3/4.

6/8 can be found in some polkas and jigs. You get "**One**-two-three **Four**-five-six".

9/8

9/8 isn't super common. The stress comes on 1, 4, and 7 giving you "**One**-two-three **Four**-five-six **Seven**-eight-nine".

12/8

12/8, however, is a pretty interesting time signature. You can find it in blues, doo-wop, and fun rock. It gives a shuffle feel. You get the stress on 1, 4, 7, and 10, giving you "**One**-two-three **Four**-five-six **Seven**-eight-nine **Ten**-eleven-twelve".

Something To Note

You may have noticed that compound time bears a resemblance to simple time. Let's compare 4/4 and 12/8.

Both 4/4 and 12/8 have 4 sets of notes… 4 quarter notes vs. 4 sets of 3 eighth notes. This isn't terribly interesting as is…

Until we turn the quarter notes in 4/4 into sets of eighth note triplets.

Now they look almost identical. That's because they really are. You could write an entire piece in 4/4 triplets and it would be indistinguishable from writing in 12/8. 12/8 is just easier to read if that's your plan (and you don't have to put '3's over every set of notes!).

This concept works for any compound time signatures. 2/2 or 2/4 eighth note triplets will feel like 6/8. 3/4 triplets will feel like 9/8.

Cool, right?

Irregular Time

Now we get to some more complex time signatures. *Irregular time* (also called Complex or Odd time) describes time signatures where the beats can't be evenly divided into 2 or 3 as they can with simple or compound time signatures.

5/4

5/4 is the most common irregular time signature you run into. It's usually grouped into 3 beats and 2 beats which gives you "**One**-two-three **Four**-five". But you'll also see that flipped to 2 and 3.

5/4 is probably most famously heard in Dave Brubeck's "Take Five".

7/4

Not as common as 5/4, but still around. 7/4 is often grouped into 4 and 3, giving you "**One**-two-three-four **Five**-six-seven". Again, it can be turned around to 3 and 4.

Pink Floyd's "Money" uses 7/4.

THE CRASH

-**Time Signatures** tell you 2 things:
> -**Bottom Number** – which note gets the beat
> -**Top Number** – how many beats per measure

-The most common types of time signatures are:
> -**Simple** - the top number is 2, 3, or 4 and you have 1 group of beats
> -**Complex** - the top number is divisible by 3 and the bottom number is probably an 8
> -**Irregular** - the beats can't be easily divided into 2 or 3

-The most common of all of these is **4/4**, aka **Common Time**

We've touched on the staff basics already, but let's dive a bit deeper!

CHAPTER 8
MORE ABOUT STAFFS

"Chapter 1" gave a quick overview of the staff. There's a *clef* that tells you which notes are on the staff, there are *lines and spaces* where the notes go, and there are *bar lines* that divide the staff into measures. Now we'll dig a bit deeper into these concepts.

> ***Quick Note!* "Staffs" *vs* "Staves"**
>
> Either is correct when talking about more than one staff. It depends largely on where you learned music and how fancy you want to sound. I opt for "staffs" simply because there's no reason to overcomplicate things... and I'm not so fancy.

Clefs

Clefs are the squiggly symbols on the far left. There are many different clefs. These are designed to keep most of the notes you play within the bounds of the staff and not too far above or below it into the *ledger lines*, which we'll discuss in a bit. Many instruments have their own clef to facilitate this. But you probably won't need most of them. So, we're just going to focus on the 2 main clefs you're likely to encounter.

Treble Clef

The treble clef is the backward "S"-looking thing on the lefthand side of the staff. This is the single most used clef you're likely to see. This clef is generally used for instruments with higher pitched notes like trumpets or female singers.

It's also called the **G Clef**. The loop toward the bottom encircles the "G" line on the staff. We'll talk more about the *notes* on the staff in a bit.

How To Draw It

 -Start with a hook, ball, or some sort of ornamentation below the staff.

 -Draw a vertical line coming off the right of that ornamentation which leans slightly left and extends up through and just above the staff.

 -From the top of the line, loop to the right and cross the vertical line at roughly the top line of the staff.

 -Continue that angled line until nearly the bottom of the staff.

 -**Here's the important part!** Encircle the second line from the bottom. This is "G". The circle should go from the first line up to the third line, then nearly back down to the first line.

Now that you've read all that, just look at the treble clef above and do your best to copy it. *Encircling "G" is really the important part.*

Bass Clef

This is the bass (pronounced: *"base"*) clef. Sort of a backward "C" with a couple dots on the righthand side. This is the second most used clef you'll run into. This clef is generally used for lower pitched instruments like tubas or male singers.

It's also called the **F Clef**. The top of the backward "C" starts, usually with a ball, on the fourth line from the bottom, which happens to be "F". More importantly, the two dots to the right of the bass clef are placed above and below that same "F" line.

How To Draw It

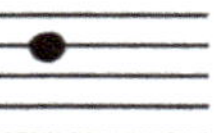 -Start with a ball on the fourth line from the bottom.

 -Curve up to the top line.

 -Continue this curve down to the bottom line so it's roughly even vertically with the edge of the ball you started with.

 -**Here's the important part!** Just to the right of the backward "C", place a dot above and a dot below the fourth line from the bottom.

And again, look at the bass clef above and do your best to copy it. *Just make sure to get those dots in there.*

Now that we know the treble and bass clefs, there's another important staff concept to know.

The Grand Staff

The grand staff combines two separate staffs together. The bar lines on the ends connect the staffs together and you have a bracket on the far left so you know it's all for one instrument. This is used for instruments, like piano, which need more notes than a single staff can provide.

Most commonly, you'll see the treble and bass staffs combined, but it doesn't have to be these two staffs.

When we get to the notes, I'll show you how they work together!

Bar Lines

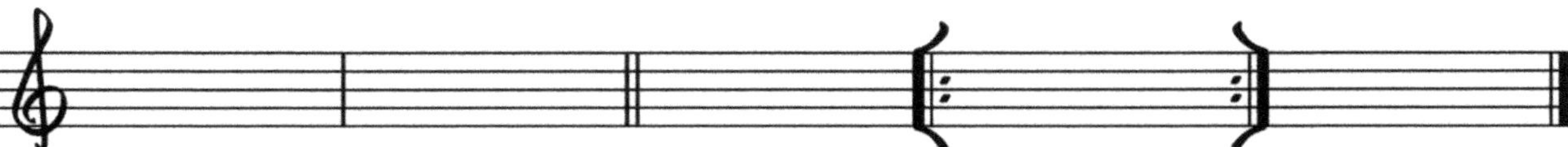

So far, we've only really touched on the fact that bar lines separate the staff into measures. That part's still true, but there are also quite a few other purposes bar lines serve. Here are the most common.

Standard

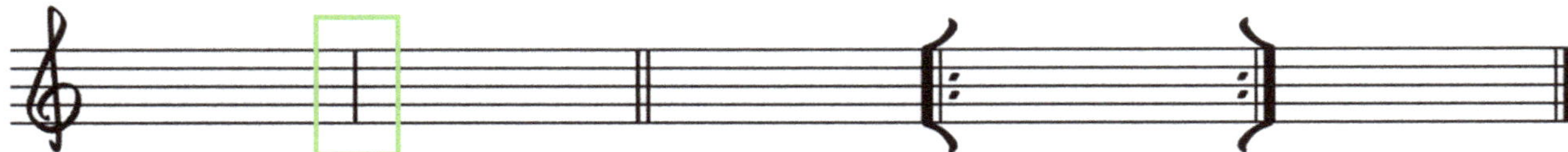

The *standard bar line* is what you'll see the most (that's why it's called "Standard"). It's the single line that separates the staff into measures.

Double

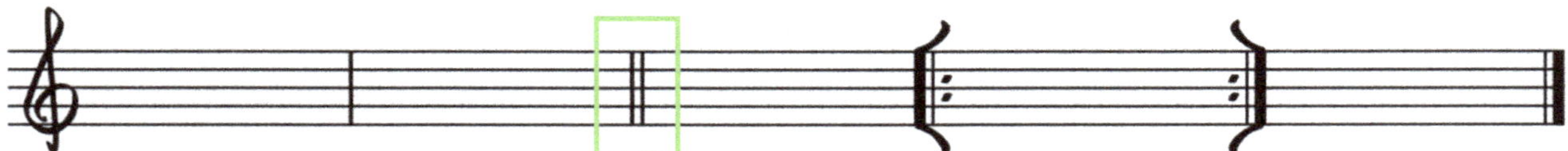

The *double bar line* isn't quite as straight forward. This is used to separate *sections of music* so it's easier to follow along. For example, it might be placed at the end of a verse before a chorus begins, separating the verse and the chorus. In most music today, you'll find a double bar line every 8 or 16 bars.

Repeat

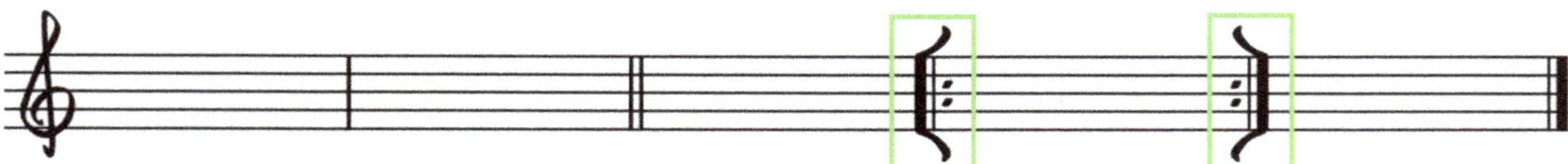

There are two *repeat bar lines* which tell you when to *begin* a repeated section and when to *end* a repeated section. The first above is the **Begin Repeat** and the second is the **End Repeat**.

If you only see an end repeat bar line in a piece, it means you need to go back to the beginning of the piece.

Unless specified, you only repeat the section between the repeat bar lines once.

End

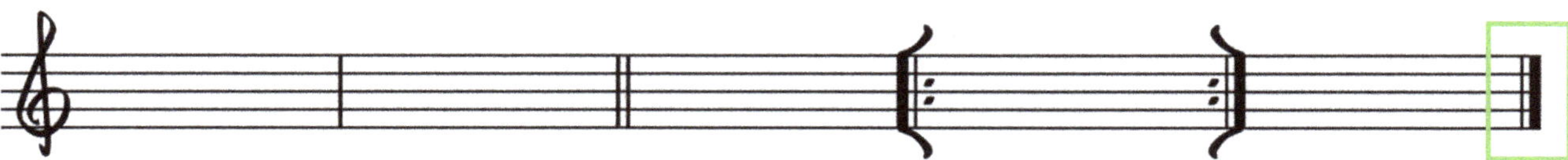

This one is probably self-explanatory, but the *end bar line* indicates the end of the song.

The Crash

Clefs

-**Clefs** are important
-The two most common clefs are **Treble Clef** and **Bass Clef**
-The **Grand Staff** combines the treble and bass clef into one unit

Bar Lines

-**Bar Lines** serve many important functions
-The most common bar lines are **Standard, Double, Repeat,** and **End**

Now let's finally learn about the actual notes on the page!

CHAPTER 9
NOTES

We've talked a lot about rhythms, but that's only one piece of the puzzle. Now let's get to what those lines and spaces on the staff are for. The notes!

The Musical Alphabet

We're all familiar with the alphabet and the whole *A to Z* thing. The musical alphabet follows that to a point.

A B C D E F G

This is the entire musical alphabet. A to G. If you need a letter beyond G you have to loop back to the beginning and start with A. It might be better represented like this.

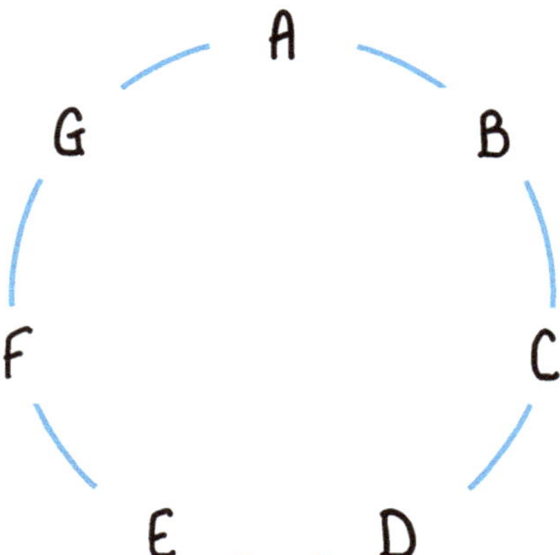

Wait, I only get seven different notes to choose from?!

Well, no. But this is what you need to know for now.

Lines and Spaces

We've talked about how there are **5 lines** and **4 spaces** on a staff. If you should ever need to count these, start from the bottom.

5 —————————
            4
4 —————————
            3
3 —————————
            2
2 —————————
            1
1 —————————

You've probably noticed I've already used this counting method to describe the positions of a few different things. It just helps everyone to be on the same page.

It's also a system that just sort of makes sense, since the *higher you go* on the staff the *higher the pitch*, and the *lower you go* the *lower the pitch*.

Okay, let's finally see how this all comes together.

Treble Staff Notes

> ### Quick Note! "Treble _Staff_" vs "Treble _Clef_"
>
> Notice I'm calling these "Treble **Staff** Notes" and not "Treble **Clef** Notes". The clef is just the symbol on the left of the staff to tell you what kind of staff you're looking at, but once it's there the staff becomes the _treble staff_ or _bass staff_ or whatever other clef you put there.

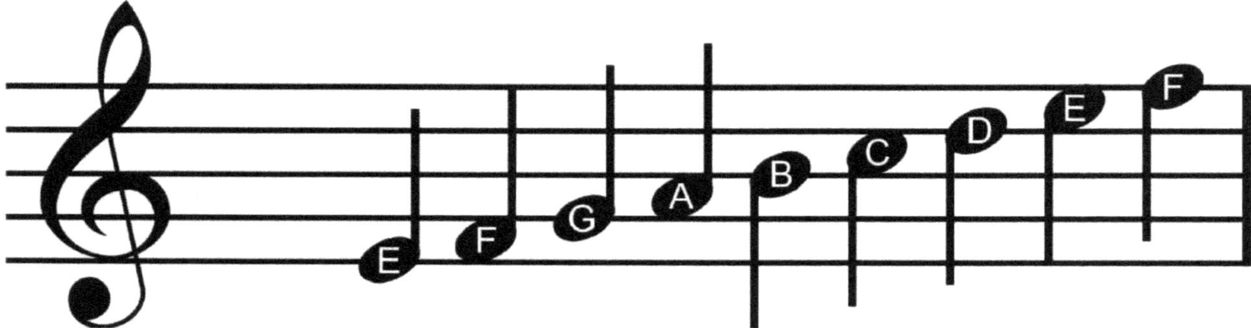

I've added the letter names to the notes for ease of understanding. You won't normally see letter names on the note heads.

The notes on the treble staff go from E to F. This can seem like a lot to remember at first glance. It's a bit easier if we break it into chunks.

Treble Staff Lines

Let's start with the note names on the lines of the treble staff:
E, G, B, D, F.

From one _line_ note to the next, a letter gets skipped between. This info becomes helpful when you get to the point of building chords. For now, let's work with an acronym to help out.

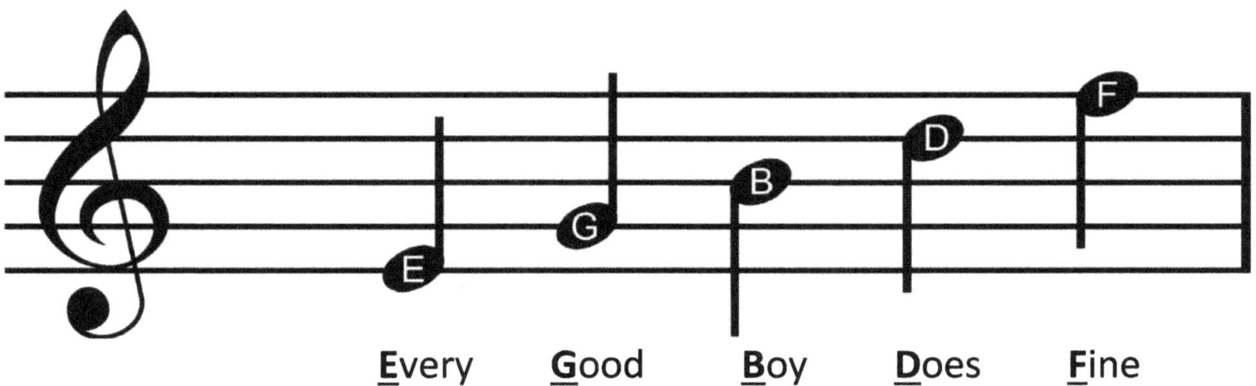

This is a common acronym for these notes, but you can always come up with your own if you're feeling creative:

Electric **G**rapes **B**reak **D**own **F**ences

Treble Staff Spaces

Now the notes on the spaces:
F, A, C, E.

Again, they skip a letter from one *space* note to the next.

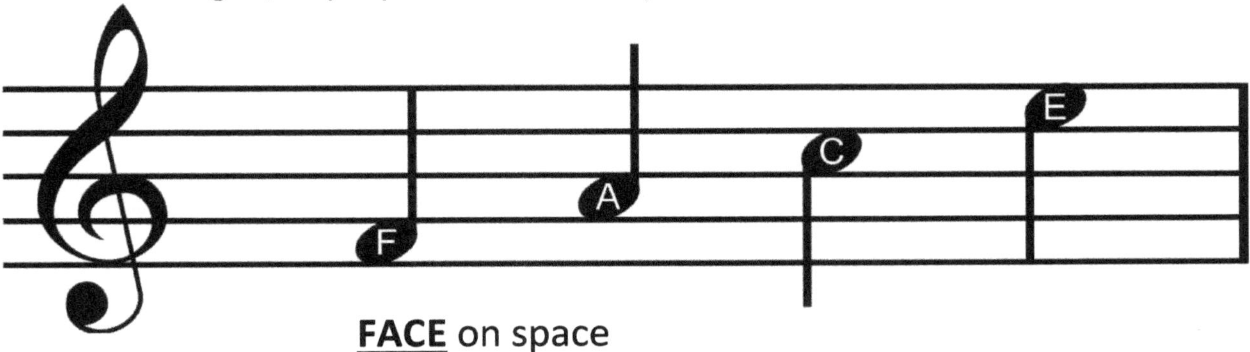

So, for the treble staff we have:

Lines = **E**very **G**ood **B**oy **D**oes **F**ine
 and
Spaces = **FACE** on space

> ### *Quick Note!* <u>Note</u> <u>Stems</u>
>
> If you look at the treble staffs above, you'll notice that the note stems (the lines coming off the sides of the noteheads) don't all go the same direction. This, as with nearly everything else, makes the music is easier to read. If the note stems all went up, they'd eventually go way above the staff.
>
> Three general rules:
>
> 1) If the note is below the third line ("B" on the treble staff), stems go up. If the note is above the third line, stems go down. If the note is on the third line, the stem goes down… but you'll often see this rule broken, so, kinda up to you.
>
> 2) If the stem goes up, it goes on the right of the notehead. If the stem goes down, it goes on the left.
>
> 3) The stem usually extends to the next note placement with the same letter. For example, the stem on a first space "F" (above) extends to the top line, which is also an "F".
>
> Again, "General Rules". These aren't set in stone.

BASS STAFF NOTES

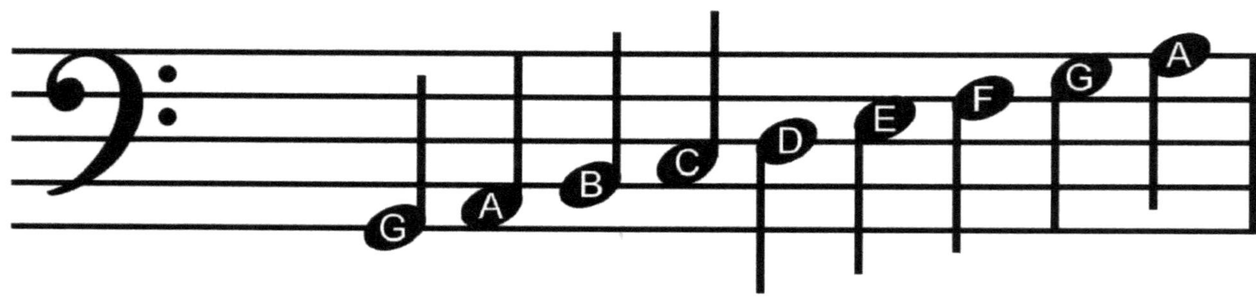

These notes go from G to A.

Bass Staff Lines

Let's start with the lines again:
G, B, D, F, A.

Like the treble staff notes, these skip a letter between. And, of course, there are more acronyms.

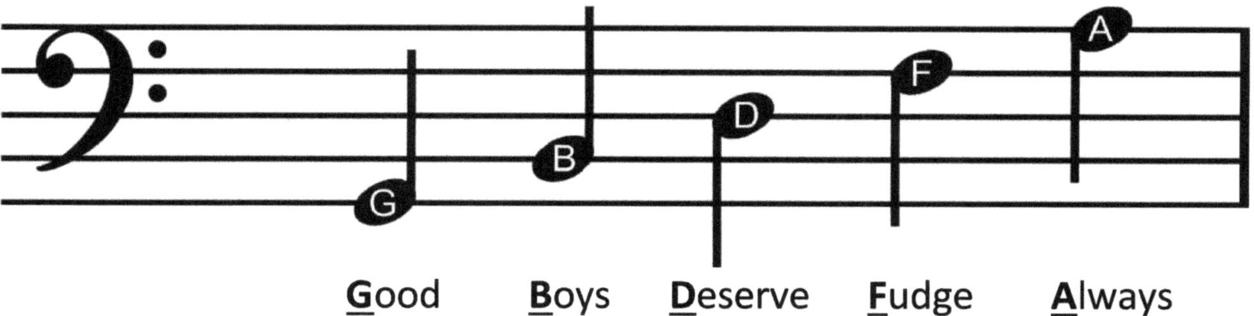

Bass Staff Spaces

Now the spaces:
A, C, E, G.

Skip letters between.

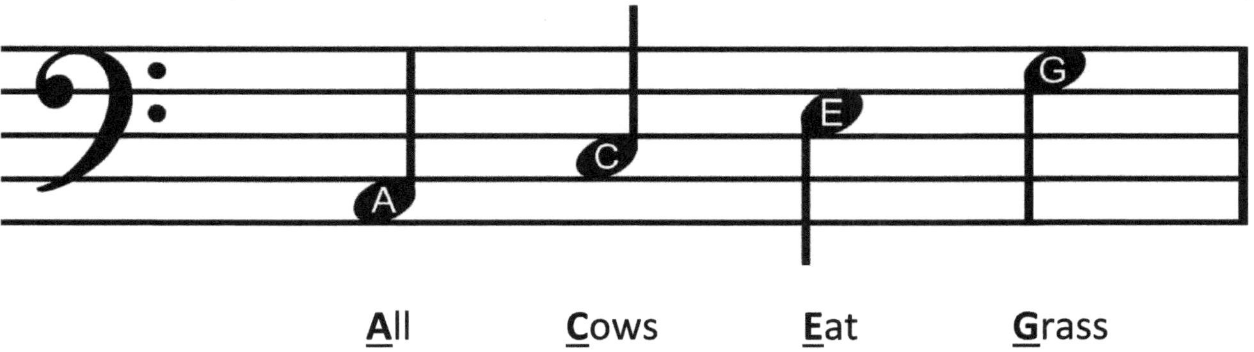

Not quite as clean as "Face on space", but "Aceg" is terrible for rhyming.

In the examples above, you may notice that there is more than one note with the same letter. Since we only have the 7 note letters in the musical alphabet, that's just the way it is. If you really want to get into the weeds, the higher notes with same letters *vibrate twice as fast* as the notes lower and sound really similar. These notes are in **octaves**. We'll get to octaves in a bit.

Can't notes go above or below the staff?

Yes, they can. Introducing, *ledger lines*!

LEDGER LINES

Ledger lines are just extended lines of the staff. They give you way more freedom regarding the range of notes you can play. They're invisible unless you have a note on a line or space above or below the staff.

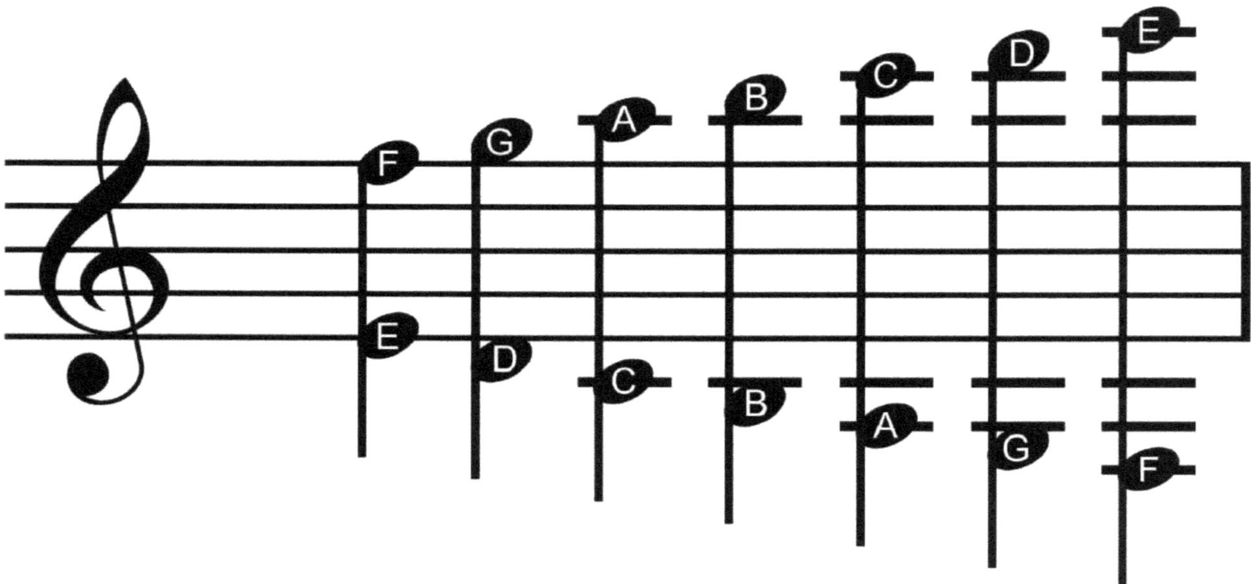

Quick Note! <u>Note</u> <u>Stems... Again</u>

You probably noticed the flagrant contradiction to the note stem 'General Rules' above. When you have more than one notehead attached to the same stem, the stem has to pick a direction.

Two general rules:

1) The stem goes the direction with the most "weight" above or below the third line. This "weight" can be the number of noteheads, the distance from the third line, or both. So, a bit subjective.

> ***Quick Note!*** <u>Note</u> <u>Stems</u>**...** <u>**Again**</u> **(cont.)**
>
> 2) If the noteheads are completely balanced (as above), the stem goes down... but, again, you'll often see this rule broken.

The notes on the ledger lines follow the same alphabetical pattern as the notes on the staff. If the notes are going up, continue forward through the musical alphabet. If the notes are going down, continue backward through the musical alphabet.

These notes can continue as far as you want them to go, but at some point you may want to consider putting those notes on a clef that will make them easier to read. People don't love reading notes too far above or below a staff.

This brings us back to the *grand staff*.

GRAND STAFF NOTES

As we learned earlier, the grand staff combines 2 staffs (often the treble and bass) to become one big staff.

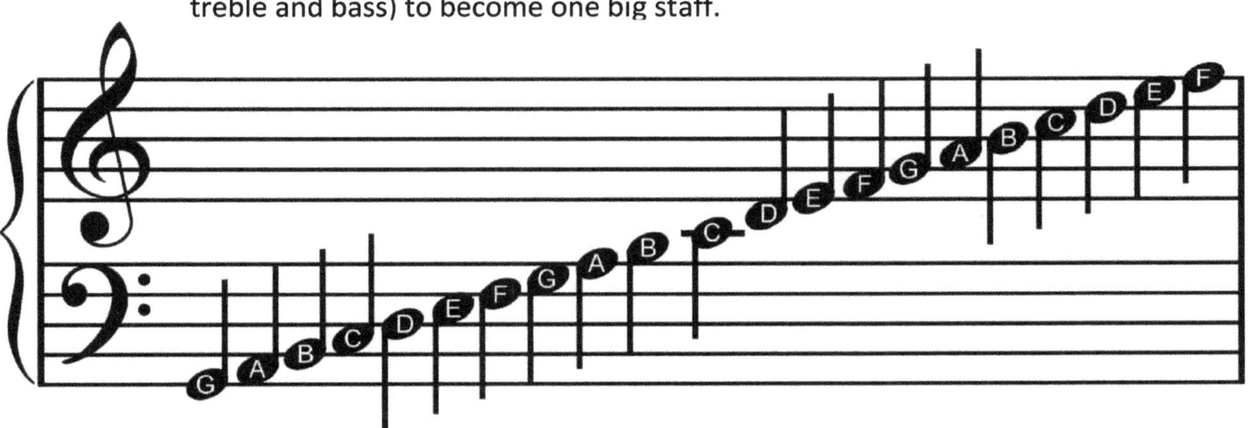

The single ledger line *above the bass staff* and *below the treble staff* is the glue that binds these two staffs together.

This is **Middle C**.

Looking at the grand staff, it's easy to see why it's called "Middle C". It's directly in the middle of the 2 staffs that make up the grand staff. All other notes on the bass staff and the treble staff are exactly the same as we've already learned.

Now let's learn about how we get more than just the 7 notes in the musical alphabet.

ACCIDENTALS

Accidentals are little symbols that raise or lower the pitch of a note.

Flat
The flat symbol looks like a lowercase "B". It flats, or **lowers the pitch,** of a note by a half-step. We'll talk about half-steps and whole-steps in a bit.

Natural
The natural symbol looks like you combined an "L" and a "7". This turns a note into its natural pitch. If it is *flat* or *sharp* for whatever reason, this will get rid of its *"flatness"* or *"sharpness"*.

Sharp
The sharp symbol looks like a hashtag or pound sign. This works like the flat symbol, but it **raises the pitch** of a note by a half-step instead of lowering it.

There are two other less common accidentals you should know about.

Double Accidentals

Double accidentals raise or lower the pitch of a note by *2 half-steps* (or 1 whole-step).

Double Flat
It's just 2 flat symbols next to each other. Simple. It lowers the pitch of a note by 2 half-steps.

Double Sharp

The design team on this one was a bit more creative. The double sharp symbol looks a bit like a fat-winged "X", or a four-leaf clover. As you can imagine, it raises the pitch of a note by 2 half-steps.

Why would I ever need to double flat _or_ double sharp _a note?_

It does seem a bit odd, right? These come into play when building chords and scales and wanting to be very specific.

Let's see what all these accidentals look like on the page.

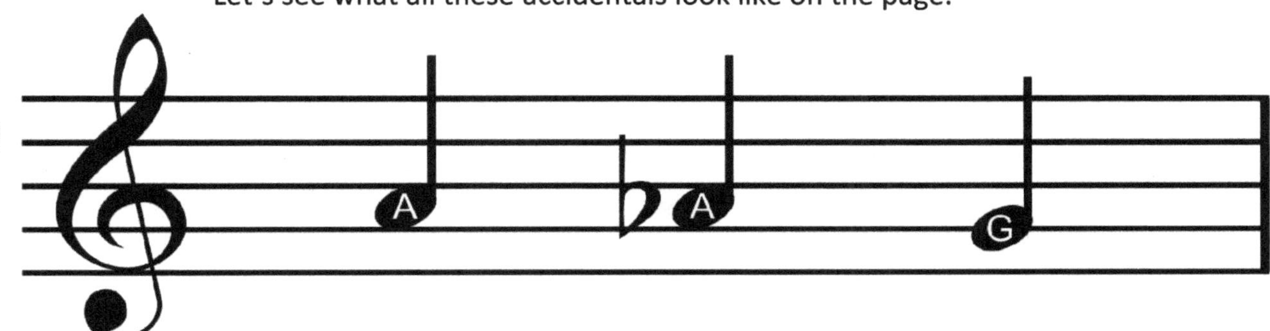

The second note above is still on the space with the "A", so you have to call it an "A". But we've added the flat symbol. So it becomes "A♭", or "*A flat*". This note lies right between "A" and "G".

The second note on this one sits on the "G" line, so it must be a "G" of some sort. The sharp symbol makes it "G♯", or "*G sharp*". This note lies right between "G" and "A".

Wait! You said "A♭" came between "G" and "A"!

I did. And it does. But so does "G♯". These notes are **enharmonic equivalents**. We'll discuss enharmonic equivalents right after our initial chat about accidentals.

Back to our "G♯". If we want the note that follows "G♯" to go back to just being "G", we have to tell it that. That's where the natural symbol comes in. Above we have "G", "G♯", "G". We went up a half-step to the "G♯", then back down a half-step to the "G" as directed by the natural symbol.

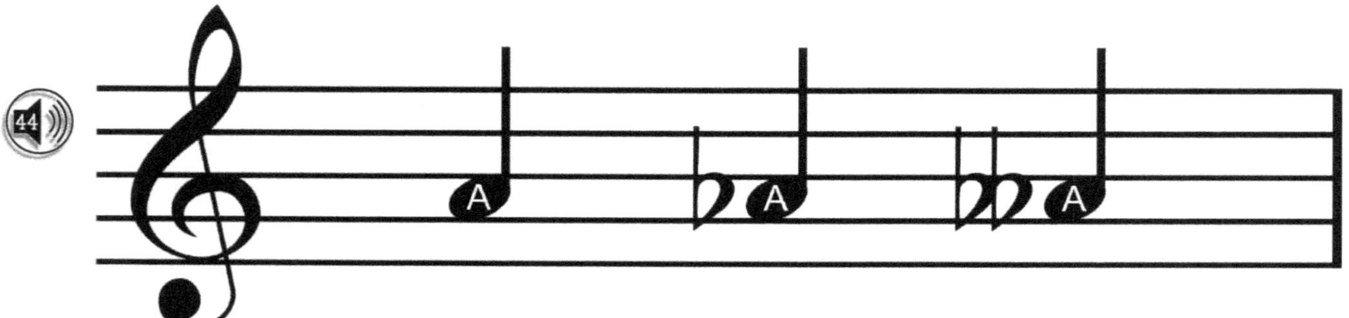

Now we get to these crazy double flats and double sharps. Since the "A" double flat is still on the "A" space, it has to be called an "A". "A" to "A♭" is down a half-step. "A♭" to "A double flat" is down a half-step. So, the passage above moves down by half-steps both times.

It works the same way with double sharps.

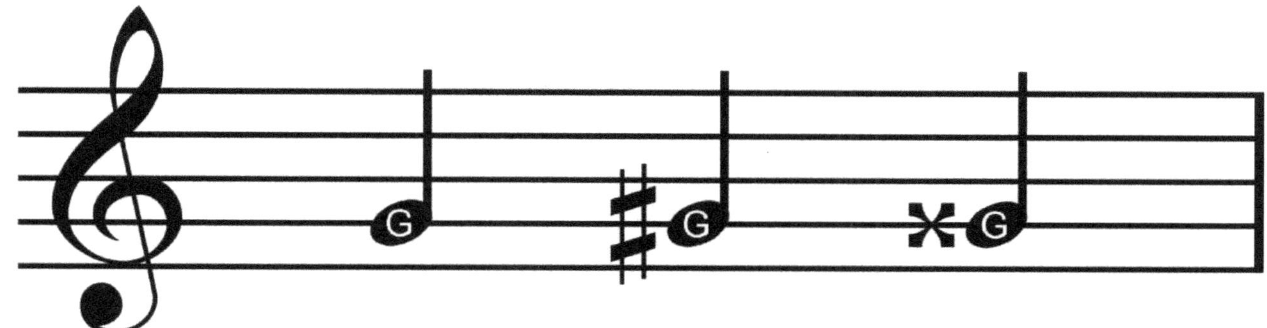

All of these notes are on the "G" line, so they all have to be some sort of "G". "G" to "G♯" is up a half-step and "G♯" to "G double sharp" is up a half-step. So, this line is moving *up* by half-steps.

RULES

As with most things in music, there are some general rules to follow here.

First, a loose rule that can be broken when you see fit:

To Flat or To Sharp?
As you probably noticed above, the "A♭" and the "G♯" both land between the "G" and the "A" and seem to be the same note.

So, when do you use one versus the other?

If your notes are moving *up*, like the "G", "G♯", "A" passage above, you want to use a *sharp*. If the notes are moving *down*, like the "A", "A♭", "G" passage above, you want to use a *flat*. It just seems to be easier to read that way.

Now, some pretty hard and fast rules you should know about.

Within A Measure

If a note has an accidental *anywhere in a measure*, the next time you run into that note in the measure it's still sharp or flat - or whichever accidental is used.

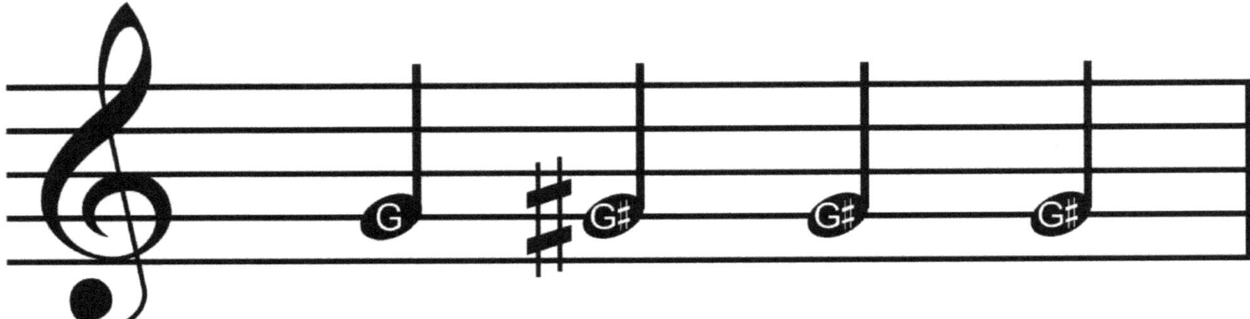

Since the note on beat 2 is "G♯", beats 3 and 4 are also "G♯.

From Measure to Measure

However, once you move to another measure, *everything resets*.

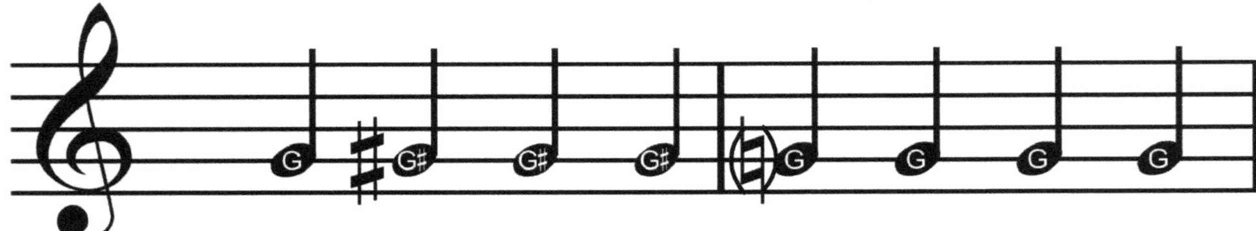

The following measure goes back to "G". You may or may not see an accidental (like the "natural symbol" in measure 2 above), but the notes will *always reset when you move to a new measure*.

Octaves – An Exception to the "Within a Measure" Rule

Remember from earlier, an octave is the same note letter a ways above or below the same note letter. When it comes to octaves, *each octave needs its own accidentals*. They're non-transferable.

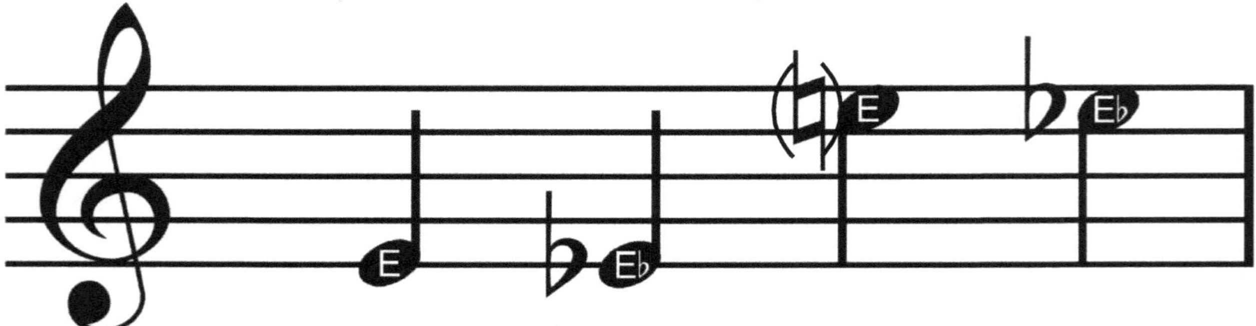

The "E♭" on beat 2 *doesn't* apply to the "E" on beat 3. Again, you may or may not see a courtesy accidental like you see on beat 3 telling you that it's natural, but if nothing changed *that note* in *that octave* earlier in the measure, you have to assume it's not changed.

Okay, now what is all this enharmonic equivalents talk?

ENHARMONIC EQUIVALENTS

Enharmonic equivalents, or, less formally, enharmonics, are two notes that *sound exactly the same*, but are *written differently*.

We talked about "G♯" and "A♭" earlier. Between "G" and "A" there is only one pitch we can use, but it can be spelled multiple ways.

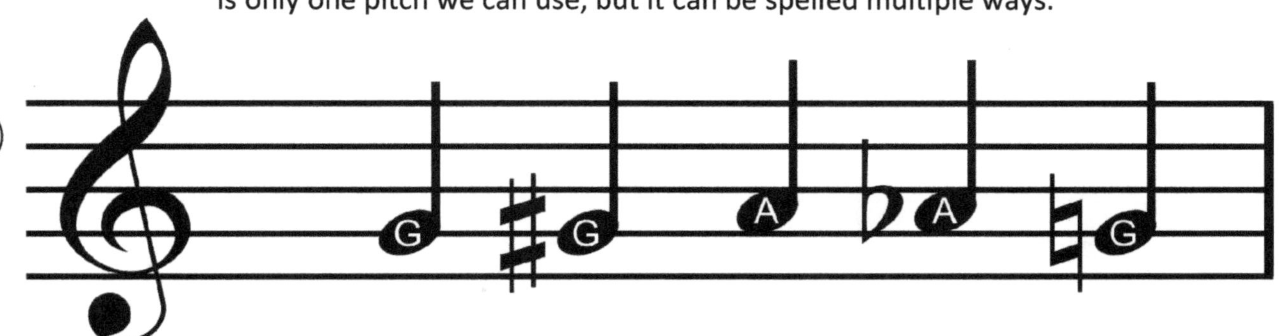

The "G♯" and the "A♭" are *enharmonic spellings* of the same pitch, the half-step between "G" and "A".

Why do this?

Like we talked about in the "Rules" section, if a passage of notes is moving up, you generally use a sharp, and if a passage is moving down, you generally use a flat. These enharmonics also become really useful when spelling out chords and scales.

Now, about these double flats and sharps.

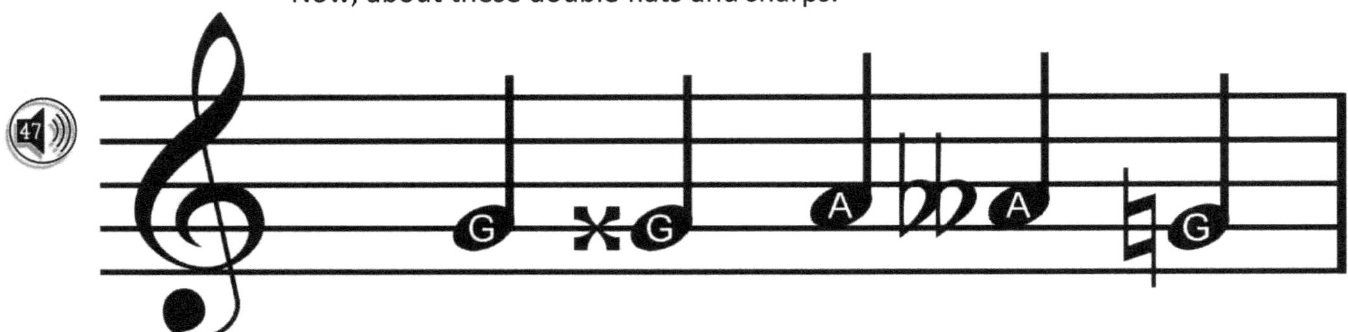

You may have realized that if there is only one possible pitch between "G" and "A", a "G double sharp" doesn't really have any room.

Well, a "G double sharp" is the enharmonic equivalent of an "A". And the "A double flat" above is the enharmonic equivalent of a "G".

So, the passage above could also be written like this:

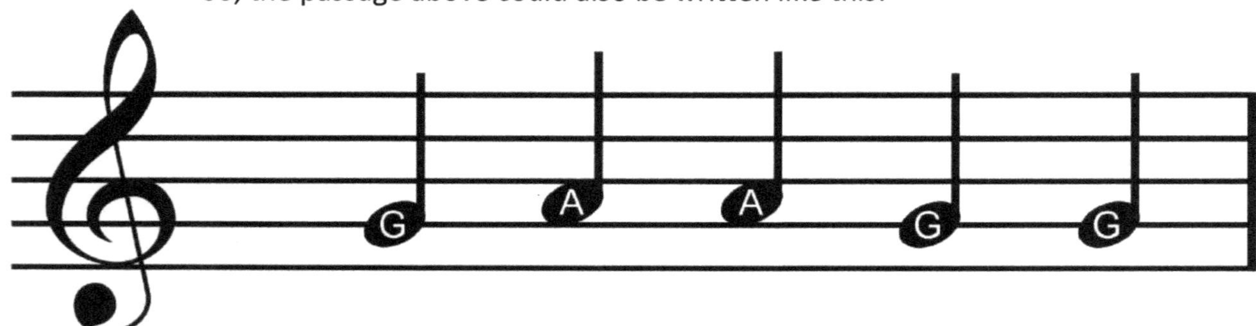

That's so confusing! Why would you ever do that??

This is pretty specific to spelling out chords and scales "correctly".

You don't often see double flats and double sharps, but you need to know what they are when you do see them.

THE CRASH

THE MUSICAL ALPHABET

-The **Musical Alphabet** is **A B C D E F G**

LINES AND SPACES

-Notes go on the lines and spaces of the staff
-The **higher** on the staff, the higher the pitch
-The **lower** on the staff, the lower the pitch

TREBLE STAFF

-**Treble Staff** notes:
Lines = **E, G, B, D, F**, or **E**very **G**ood **B**oy **D**oes **F**ine
Spaces = **F, A, C, E**, or **FACE** on space

BASS STAFF

-**Bass Staff** notes:
Lines = **G, B, D, F, A**, or **G**ood **B**oys **D**eserve **F**udge **A**lways
Spaces = **A, C, E, G**, or **A**ll **C**ows **E**at **G**rass

-**Ledger Lines** extend the staff above or below

-The **Grand Staff** combines the **Treble** and **Bass** staffs at **Middle C**

-**Accidentals** raise or lower the pitch of the note

-**Enharmonic Equivalents** are the same pitch spelled differently

Phew, that was a lot.

Well, buckle up. It only gets to be a lot more as we go!

CHAPTER 10
SCALES

A scale is a series of pitches that go *in order*, either up or down the musical alphabet, and begin and end on the same note (so none of the middle note letters repeat). Scales are essential to understanding how chords are built. There are many different scales to choose from, but we'll keep it fairly simple here. We'll deal with the major scale, the basic minor scales (yup, there are multiple), the chromatic scale, and the whole-tone scales.

But before we do that, we need to talk about half-steps and whole-steps. And before we even do that, let's get familiar with the piano keys.

The Piano Keys

I've added the note names to help you along.

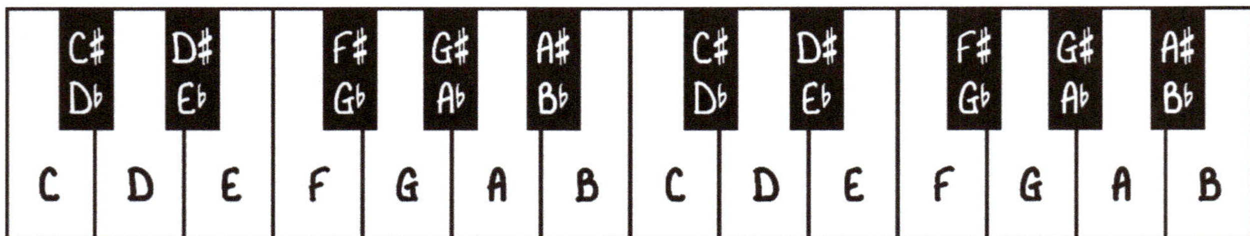

There are *white keys* and *black keys*. Each piano key gets a letter name.

The white keys are separated by **sets of 2 black keys** and **sets of 3 black keys**. These black keys are where the *accidentals* generally come in.

The *white key* before the sets of *2 black keys* will always be a "C" and the *white key* before the sets of *3 black keys* will always be an "F". This can help you orient yourself to the keyboard to help you find the other notes.

The white keys correspond to the *natural notes* on the staff.

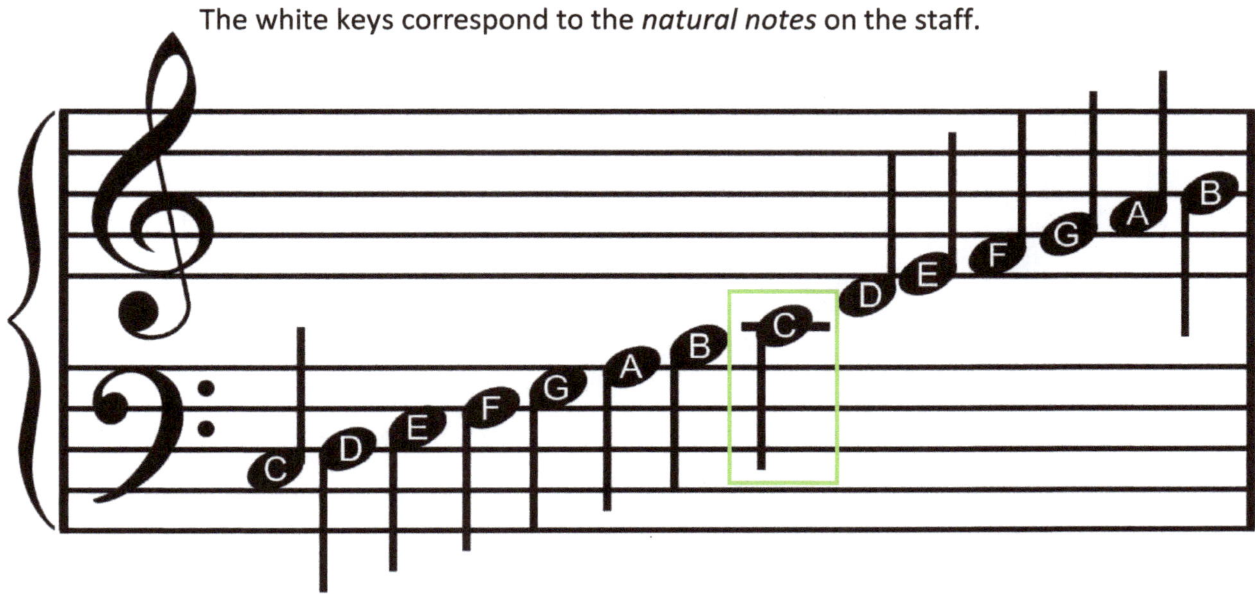

Notice that the "C" on the ledger line between the treble staff and the bass staff is in the *middle of the keyboard*. Middle C!

Now let's get down to this half-step and whole-step business.

HALF-STEPS & WHOLE-STEPS

Half-steps and whole-steps refer to the distance from one note to the next.

Half-Steps

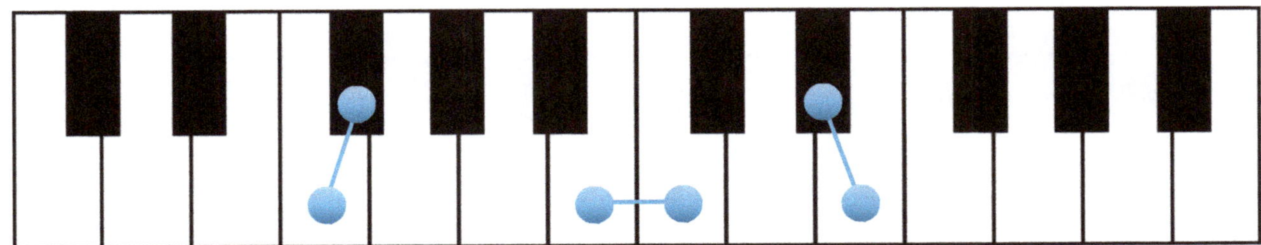

<u>Half-steps</u> are the distance *from one piano key to the adjacent key*. It doesn't matter if you're going from a white key to a black key, a white key to a white key, or a black key to a white key. As long as it's the *very next piano key*, it's a <u>half-step</u>.

Whole-Steps

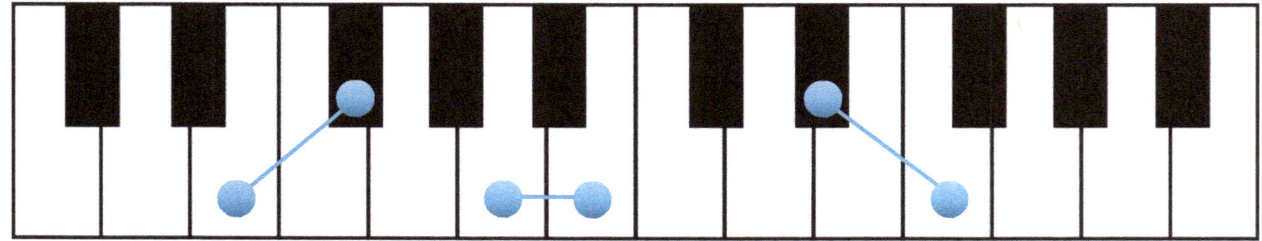

<u>Whole-steps</u>, as you can imagine, are *2 half-steps*. Again, it doesn't matter what color the keys are; move 2 half-steps and you've gone a <u>whole-step</u>.

It also doesn't matter which direction you go. Up the keyboard or down the keyboard, <u>half-steps</u> are the next key, <u>whole-steps</u> are 2 half-steps.

Okay, now that we've got that out of the way, we can finally build scales!

Major Scale

The major scale is going to be the one you find useful for most music. It's not necessarily the most glamorous, but it's the workhorse that does a lot of the heavy lifting.

Let's go back to our piano.

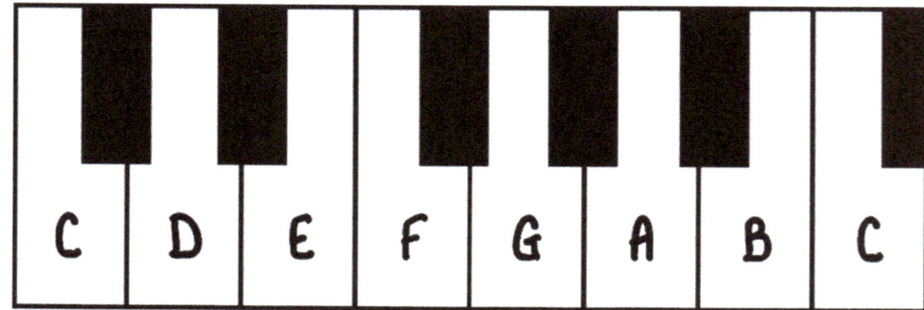

If you start on "C" and play just the white keys up to the next "C", you've played the *C Major Scale*. Congratulations! First scale in the bag!

But what makes this a major scale?

Okay, let's dissect it a bit. First, most scales you'll be using consist of **7 notes + the octave.** 8 notes total. These 8 notes follow a pattern. Bring in our half-steps and whole-steps.

Let's call a whole-step "W", and a half-step "H".

Major Scale = **WWH WWWH**

What?!

Let's stick with the C Major Scale:
"C" to "D" = whole-step
"D" to "E" = whole-step
"E" to "F" = *half-step*
"F" to "G" = whole-step
"G" to "A" = whole-step
"A" to "B" = whole-step
"B" to "C" = *half-step*.

C Major Scale = **WWH WWWH** = C D E F G A B C
(whole, whole, half,   whole, whole, whole, half)

the space in the formula above is just there to help remember the pattern

You can start on ANY note and use this formula to come up with a major scale.

Let's try a couple.

Starting on "G".

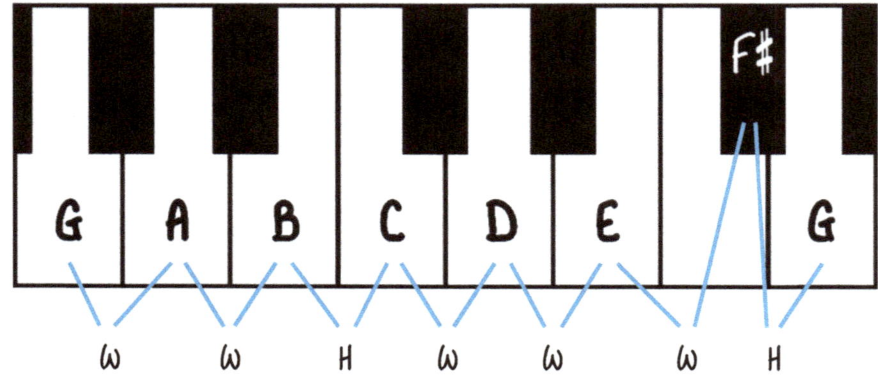

G Major Scale = **WWH WWWH** = G A B C D E F# G

Let's try a trickier one.

Starting on A♭.

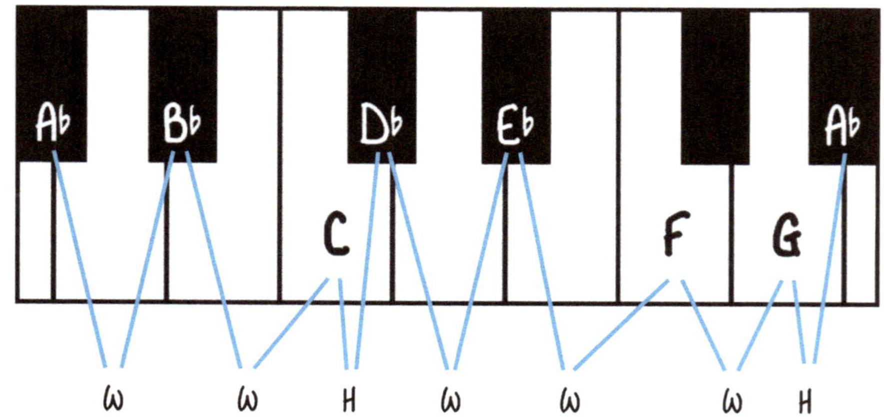

A♭ Major Scale = **WWH WWWH** = A♭ B♭ C D♭ E♭ F G A♭

If you're building a **major scale**, remember: **WWH WWWH**.

You've got the formula. Now we're going to add something else to the mix.

SCALE DEGREES

Have you heard the "Do-Re-Mi" song from *The Sound of Music*? You know, "Do, a deer"? I'm gonna guess probably (if not, take a minute to look it up). That song lays out *solfège* (or *solfeggio*):

Do, Re, Mi, Fa, Sol, La, Ti, Do

These syllables relate to the scale degrees of the major scale. It can be very valuable, but it's also one more thing to learn. Instead, we're going to work with a numbering system since most people can already count to 8.

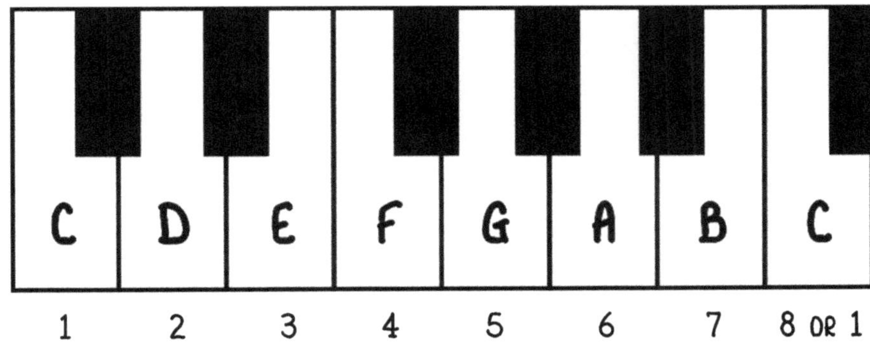

Let's see what that looks like on the treble staff.

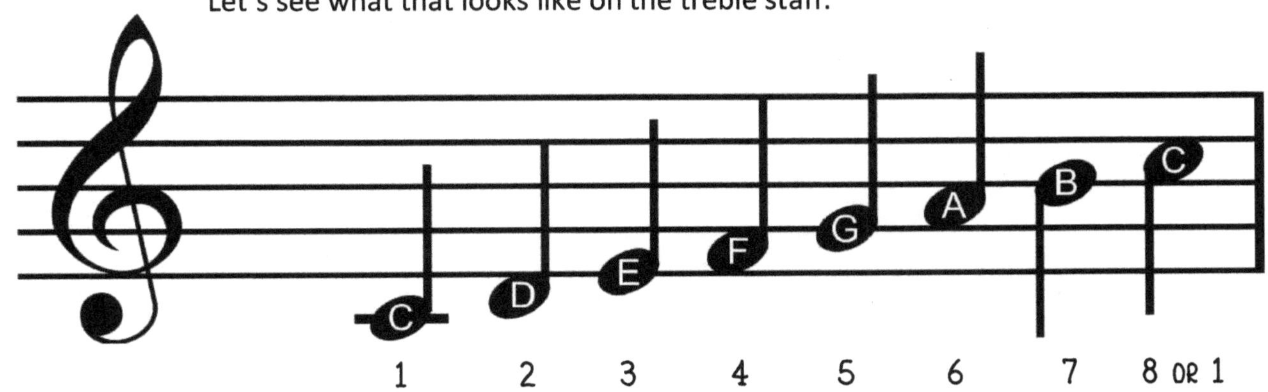

With the C Major Scale, "C" is 1. The "1" of a scale is also called the **Tonic.** Then you use your formula, **WWH WWWH**, and continue counting up the numbers. Each note gets the next number. So, D=2, E=3, and so on. "C" can also be considered 8, which is the *octave*... 8 = "Oct". See how that comes together!

This system lays out the scale degrees perfectly for you. "D" is the *2nd scale degree*. "G" is the *5th scale degree*. "B" is the *7th scale degree*.

How does this help me?

It will help immensely when we get to intervals and you eventually move onto chords. If you can understand this concept now, building chords will be much easier later.

Let's move onto our first *minor scale*.

NATURAL MINOR SCALE

Minor scales add some moodiness to your paintbox of possibilities. The first minor scale we'll look at is the *Natural Minor Scale*. It's called "natural" because it naturally occurs without having to alter any of the pitches in any way. This will make more sense when we compare the minor scales in a bit.

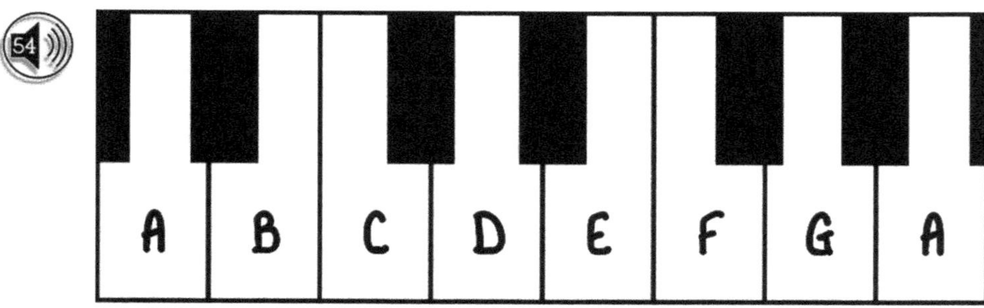

Start on "A" and play just the *white keys* up to the next "A". You just played the *A Natural Minor Scale*. Boom! First minor scale done!

Back to our whole-steps and half-steps.

Natural Minor Scale = **WH WWH WW**
(whole, half,   whole, whole, half,   whole, whole)

Again, with this formula you can start anywhere on the piano and create a natural minor scale.

Natural Minor Scale = **WH WWH WW**

Let's do one more.

Start on "C".

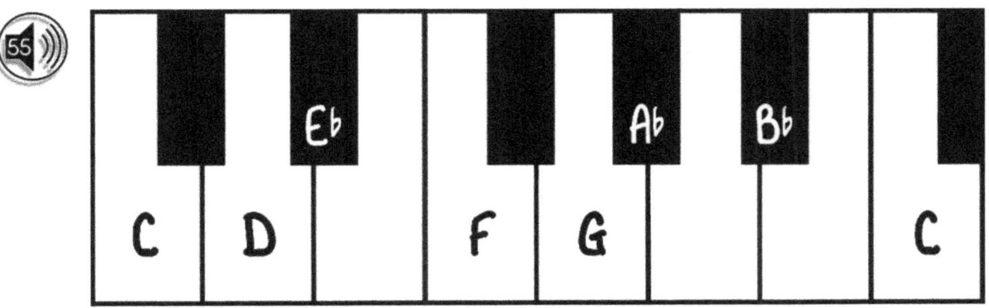

C Natural Minor Scale = **WH WWH WW** = C D Eb F G Ab Bb C

Let's look at that on the treble staff.

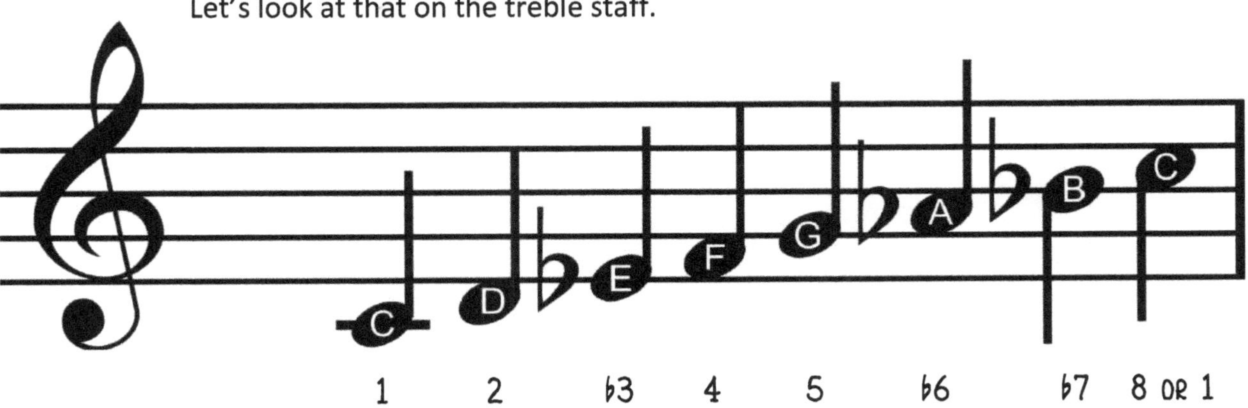

The *C Natural Minor Scale* looks an awful lot like the *C Major Scale*, doesn't it? They both start and end on "C" and have quite a few notes in common.

These are **Parallel Scales.**

They're parallel because they both start and end on the same note. They have the same "1" (in this case that note is "C"). Let's look at the similarities and differences between these parallel major and natural minor scales.

Major   = C D **E** F G **A** **B** C = 1 2 **3** 4 5 **6** **7** 8
Natural Minor = C D E♭ F G A♭ B♭ C = 1 2 ♭**3** 4 5 ♭**6** ♭**7** 8

There are 3 notes that distinguish the two. The 3/♭3 (pronounced "flat 3"), 6/♭6 ("flat 6"), and 7/♭7 ("flat 7").

Quick Note! <u>**Scale Degree Numbering**</u>

Scale degrees are based on the *major scale's numbers*. The major scale gives us 1 2 3 4 5 6 7 8. All other scales then *relate to the major scale*, which is why the natural minor scale has a ♭3, ♭6, and ♭7, because they're flatted compared to the major scale.

You will sometimes see people number minor scales as 1 2 3 4 5 6 7 8, but you have to know which notes are supposed to be altered. I find that confusing. So, we're numbering all other scales *as compared to the major scale*.

Back to the 'A' Natural Minor.

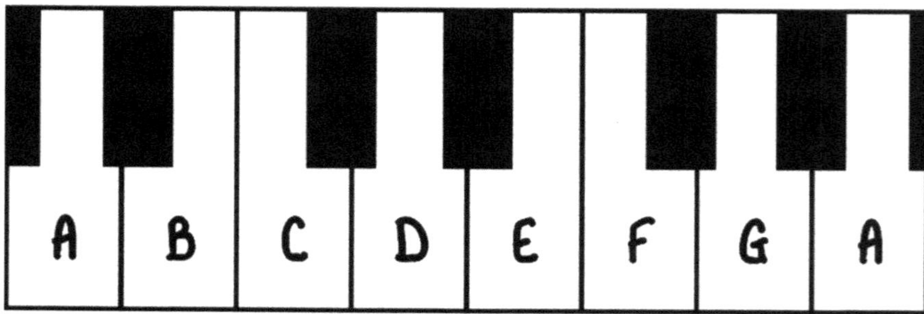

'A' Natural Minor Scale = **WH WWH WW** = A B C D E F G A

Let's look at it on the treble staff.

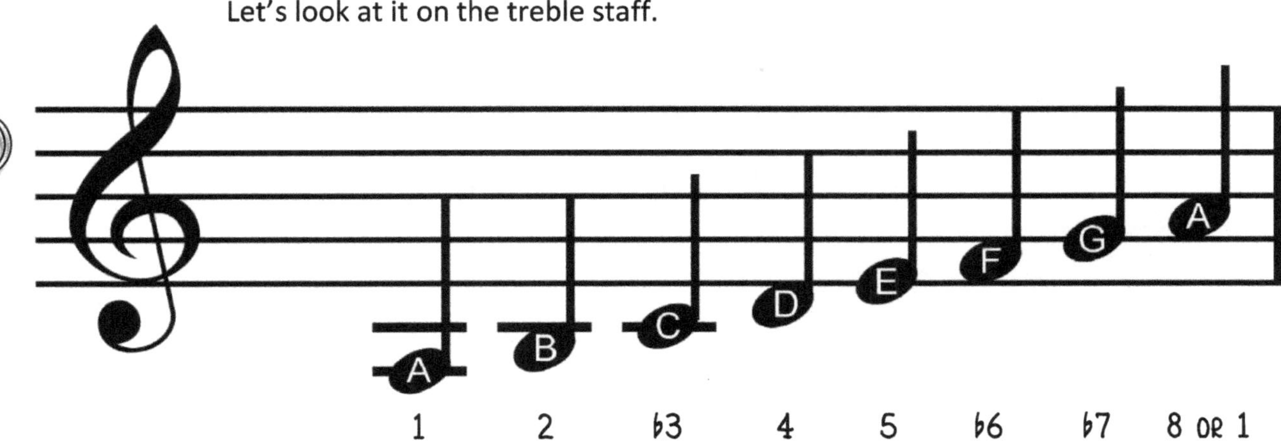

The 'A' Natural Minor Scale follows the same formula - **WH WWH WW** - as all other natural minor scales, but if you look at the piano above, you'll notice that it's played on *all white keys* just like the C Major Scale.

The 'A' Natural Minor Scale is the **Relative Minor Scale** of C Major.

A relative minor scale starts on the *6th scale degree* of the major scale it's related to. "A" is the 6th scale degree of the C Major Scale (going from major to minor, you can also think down a minor 3rd, or 3 half-steps. 3 half-steps down from "C" is "A").

Other Minor Scales

We've looked at the minor scale which occurs *naturally* if you start on the 6th scale degree of the major scale, Natural Minor. There are 2 other minor scales I'd like to touch on.

Harmonic Minor Scale

The harmonic minor scale is nearly identical to the natural minor scale, with one really important distinction... *the 7th scale degree is raised*.

Let's continue using 'A' Minor as our example.

'A' Natural Minor

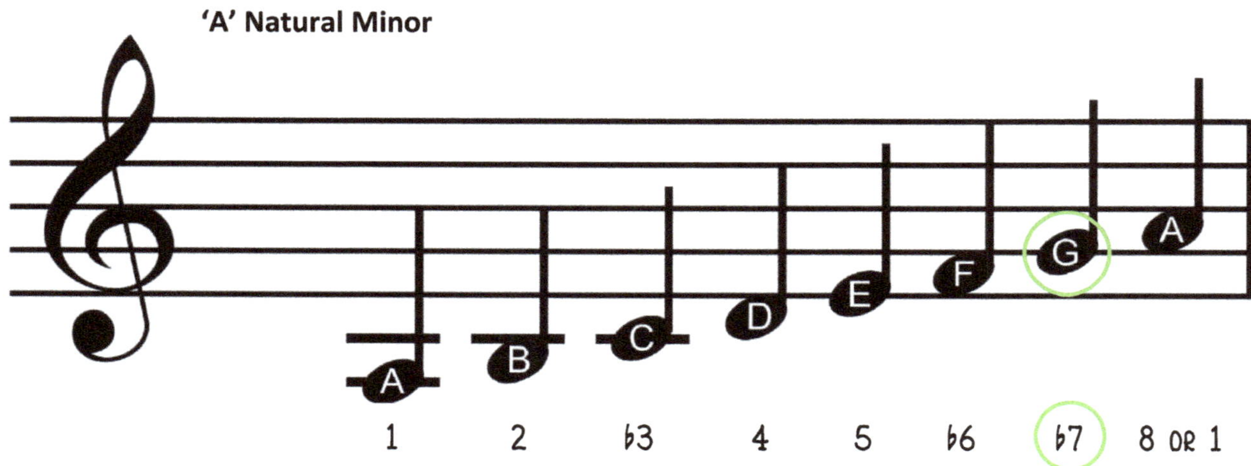

Becomes:
'A' Harmonic Minor

This is the version of the minor scale you'll generally use.

Why harmonic minor instead of the natural minor?

Without getting too far into it here, the raised 7th scale degree is important in creating a chord in minor music which gives direction to the music our ears have come to rely on.

Let's compare the natural minor to the harmonic minor.

Natural Minor = A B C D E F **G**   A = 1 2 ♭3 4 5 ♭6 ♭7 8
Harmonic Minor = A B C D E F **G♯**   A = 1 2 ♭3 4 5 ♭6 ♮7 8

Pretty similar, but that *raised 7th* will make all the difference.

One more minor scale to look at.

Melodic Minor Scale

Some people think the distance between the 6th and 7th scale degrees of the harmonic minor scale is awkward, especially for vocalists. So, they came up with the *melodic minor scale* to compensate for that. Instead of just having a raised 7th from the natural minor, *we also have a raised 6th*.

Let's start with the 'A' Natural Minor Scale.

'A' Natural Minor

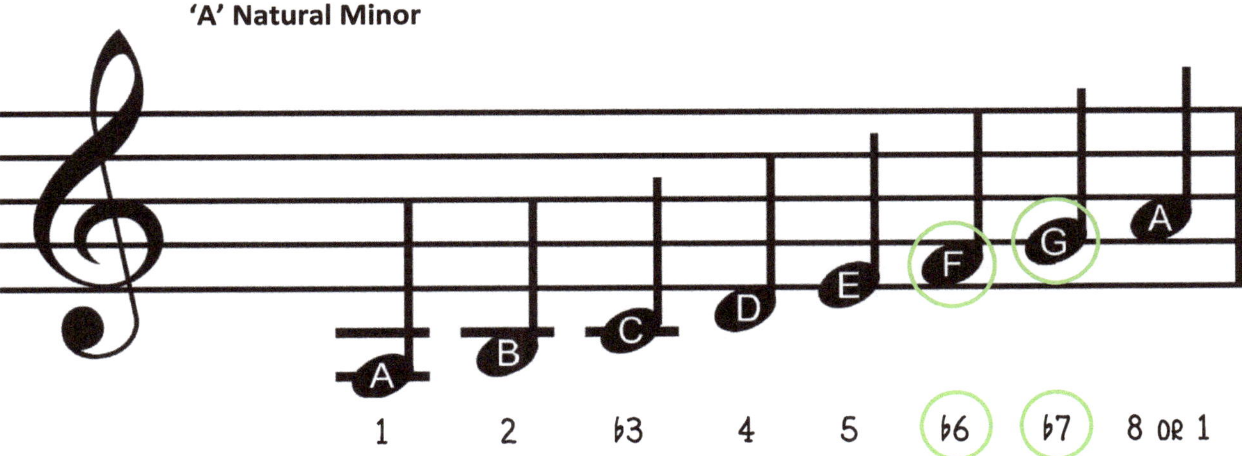

Becomes:
'A' Melodic Minor

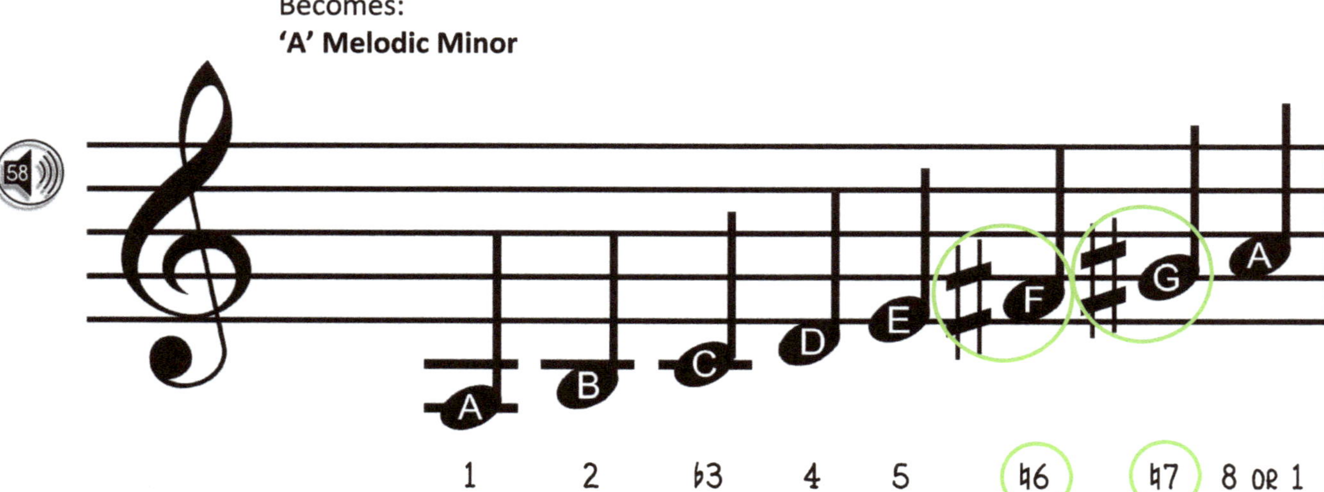

Let's compare these 3 minor scales.

Natural Minor = A B C D E **F   G** A = 1 2 ♭3 4 5 ♭6 ♭7 8
Harmonic Minor = A B C D E **F   G♯** A = 1 2 ♭3 4 5 ♭6 ♮7 8
Melodic Minor = A B C D E **F♯ G♯** A = 1 2 ♭3 4 5 ♮6 ♮7 8

You'll notice that *the first 5 notes are the same* in all 3 of these minor scales. It's only the *6th* and *7th scale degrees* that get altered in some way.

One Quick Wrench in the Melodic Minor Scale

The melodic minor scale actually has *2 forms*. **Ascending** (*going up the scale*) and **Descending** (*going down the scale*). I guess someone thought this was better for melody writing.

Ascending Melodic Minor

This is the version we just learned (with the raised 6th and 7th scale degrees):

Ascending Melodic Minor = A B C D E **F♯ G♯** A = 1 2 ♭3 4 5 ♮6 ♮7 8

Descending Melodic Minor

You've actually already learned this one! The descending melodic minor scale is the same as the natural minor scale.

Descending Melodic Minor (*Natural Minor*) =
A **G F** E D C B A = 8 ♭**7** ♭**6** 5 4 ♭3 2 1

So, that gives us:

 Ascending Melodic Minor = 1 2 ♭3 4 5 ♮**6** ♮**7** 8
Descending Melodic Minor = 8 ♭**7** ♭**6** 5 4 ♭3 2 1

Let's look at these melodic minor scales on the treble staff.

'A' Ascending Melodic Minor

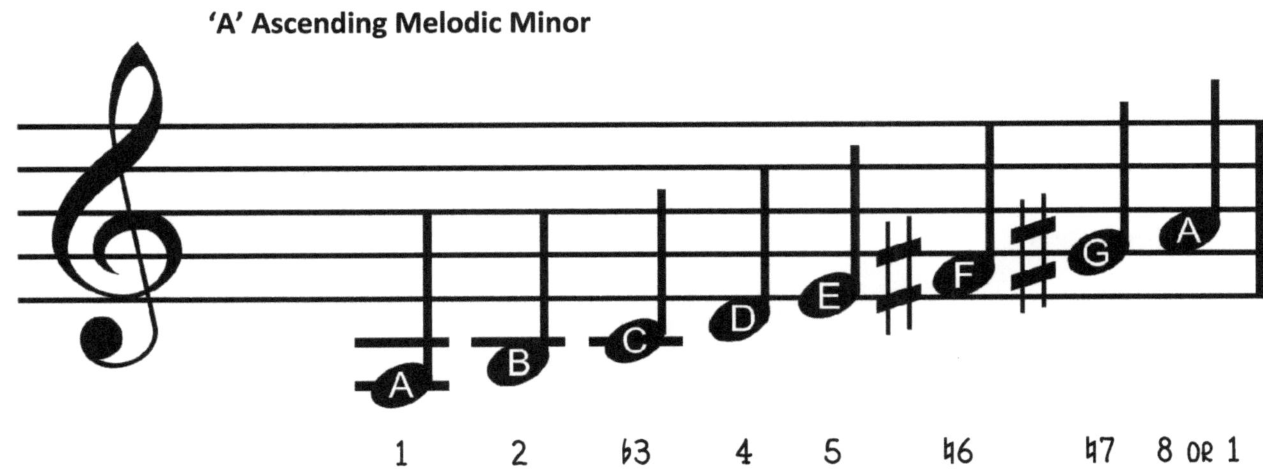

'A' Descending Melodic Minor

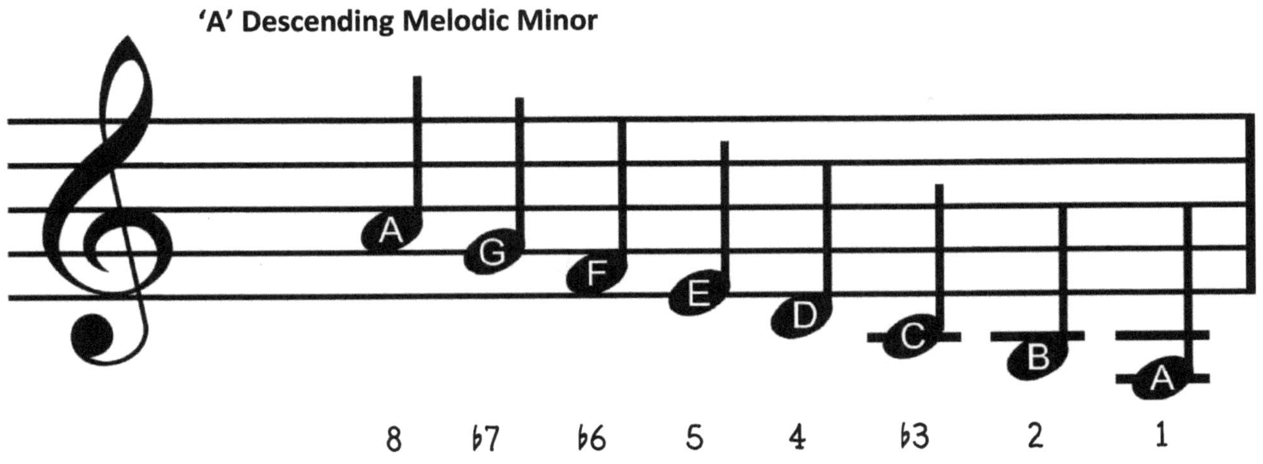

> ### *Quick Note!* <u>Melodic Minor</u>
>
> This "Ascending" vs "Descending" business was traditionally used in classical music, but it's not really a hard and fast rule. Many people just think of the "ascending melodic minor scale" as *the melodic minor scale* and completely disregard the idea of descending with the natural minor scale. So, when you write your own music, you can decide on a case-by-case basis how you want to descend…

The above scales all contain some variation of 7 pitches and are considered **tonal** scales, meaning they're played based on a tonal center, or a note considered to be "1", the tonic.

The last 2 scales I want to mention are **atonal** by nature, meaning they don't really have a "1" to return to (they also happen to be **symmetrical scales**, meaning they *divide up the octave equally*).

CHROMATIC SCALE

The first of these is the **Chromatic Scale**. The chromatic scale starts on any pitch and *moves in half-steps* to hit all the piano keys along the way; 12 notes all told.

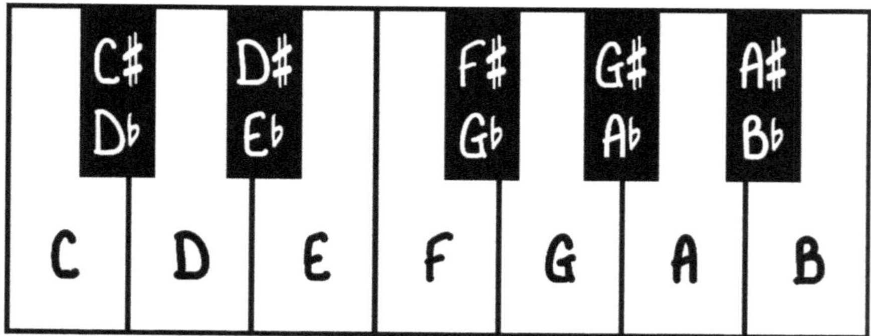

There's no specific note you need to start on or end on. It's the same scale no matter where you begin.

Let's see this on the treble staff. I'm going to decide to start on "C" like the piano above, and since I'm going to ascend (go up the notes) I'm going to use the sharp notes to demonstrate.

The chromatic scale uses all the available notes.

WHOLE-TONE SCALES

The next scale is the **Whole-Tone Scale**. This one is also atonal. Where the chromatic scale uses half-steps for the entire scale, the whole-tone scale, as you may have guessed, uses whole-steps. Since it uses whole-steps, there are actually *2 versions of this scale*.

Let's think of one of them starting on "C" and the other starting on "C#" (though, like the chromatic scale, we can start on any note).

C Whole-Tone Scale

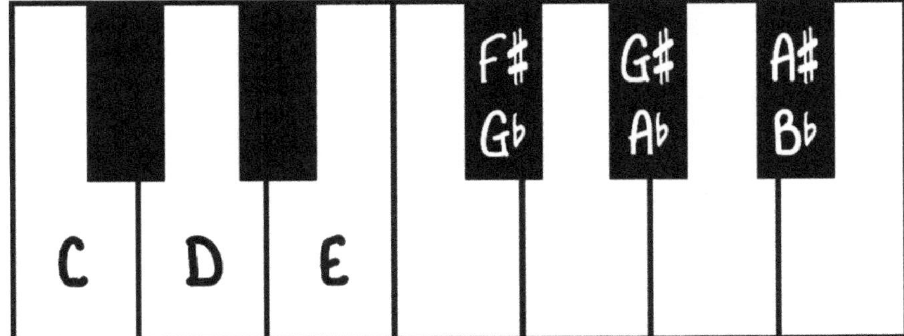

Whole-tone scales have 6 pitches to choose from, but you can start on any of those 6 pitches.

The *C Whole-Tone Scale* uses C, D, E, F#(Gb), G#(Ab), and A#(Bb).

You'll notice we skipped a note between each of those pitches.

C♯ Whole-Tone Scale

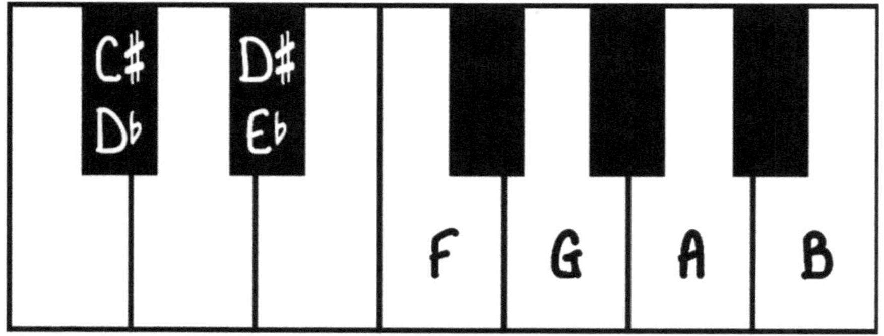

The C♯ whole-tone scale uses the other 6 pitches.

The C♯ Whole-Tone Scale uses C♯(D♭), D♯(E♭), F, G, A, and B.

If you stack those 2 whole-tone scales on top of each other we'd be back to the chromatic scale!

C Whole-Tone Scale = C		D		E		F♯		G♯		A♯	
C♯ Whole-Tone Scale =	C♯		D♯		F		G		A		B
Chromatic Scale = C	C♯	D	D♯	E	F	F♯	G	G♯	A	A♯	B

THE CRASH

-**Half-Steps** are right next to each other on the piano
-**Whole-Steps = 2 Half-Steps**

MAJOR SCALE

-**Major Scale = WWH WWWH**

-The **Scale Degrees** of the major scale are **1 2 3 4 5 6 7 8(1)**

All other scales' scale degrees are in reference to the major scale

MINOR SCALES

-**Minor Scale = WH WWH WW**

-The **Minor Scale** has 3 forms:
    Natural Minor   = 1 2 ♭3 4 5 ♭6 ♭7 8(1)
    Harmonic Minor = 1 2 ♭3 4 5 ♭6 ♮7 8(1)

    Melodic Minor has 2 forms:
        Ascending Melodic Minor = 1 2 ♭3 4 5 ♮6 ♮7 8(1)
        Descending Melodic Minor = Natural Minor

OTHER SCALES

-The **Chromatic Scale** moves in **half-steps** and uses all **12 pitches**

-The **Whole-Tone Scale** has 2 forms that move in **whole-steps** and use **6 pitches**:
    #1 = C   D   E F♯(G♭) G♯(A♭) A♯(B♭)
    #2 = C♯(D♭) D♯(E♭) F G   A   B

I know it seems like a lot, but once you dial in these scales, everything in music becomes way easier.

Now we're going to break down these scales a bit.

CHAPTER 11
INTERVALS

Intervals are the *distance between the pitches*. Knowing how to name and deal with intervals becomes crucial when you start to construct chords and melodies.

Harmonic vs Melodic

Though the actual intervals (*distance between the notes*) are the same, there are 2 ways to think about intervals.

Harmonic Intervals

Harmonic intervals are *intervals within a chord*. These intervals are thought of as being *vertical* since the notes stack on top of each other.

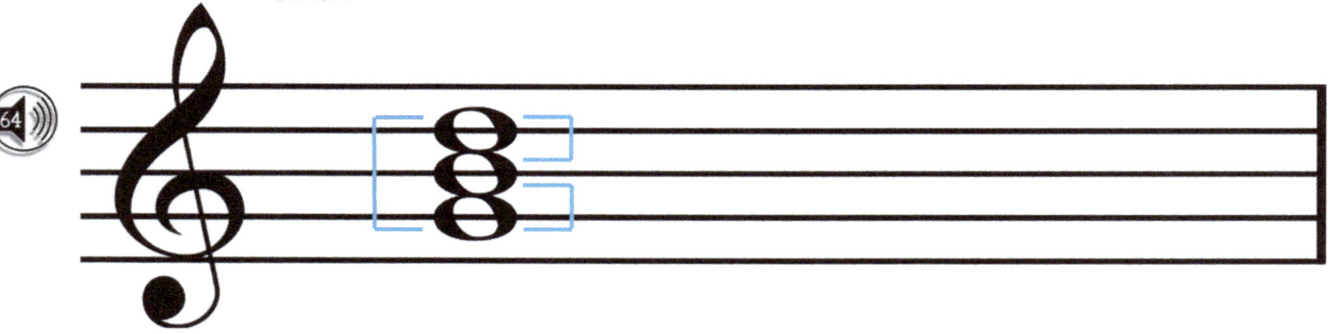

Melodic Intervals

Melodic intervals aren't necessarily part of a chord. They *move in succession* and are thought to be *horizontal*.

The two examples above show the same set of *intervals*, but you can see the clear distinction in how they're being used.

Perfect and Major Intervals

There are **5 Qualities** of interval we'll go over. We'll start with the two most basic of these intervals, **Perfect** and **Major**. Let's use the C Major Scale as our reference point.

This is how we've been looking at the C Major Scale. The intervals in this would be considered *melodic*. The scale degrees become really useful when talking about the intervals, because they are the same thing!

This is really easy to see if we turn these *melodic intervals* into *harmonic intervals*.

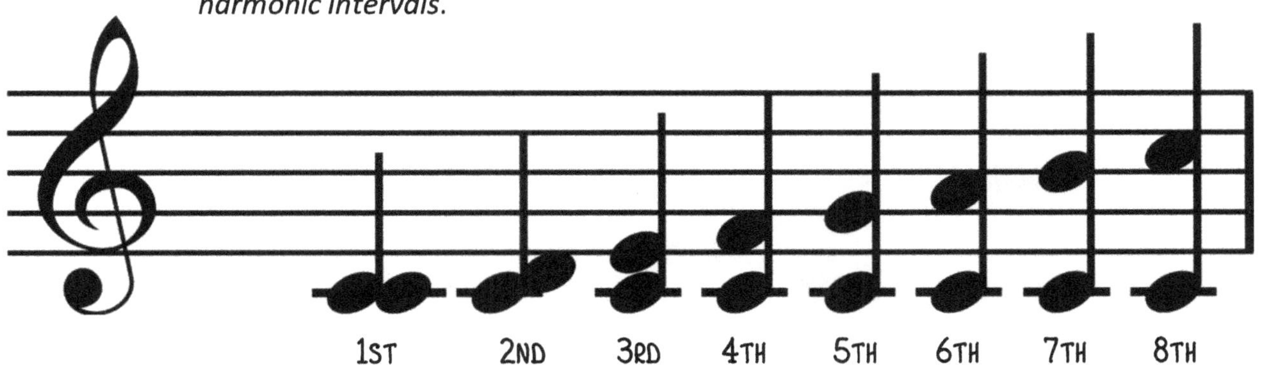

Much easier, right?

But what gives the intervals these names?

It's the distance from one note to the next. *When in a major scale,* the distance from the '1' to the '2' is a '2nd'. The distance from the '1' to the '3' is a '3rd'. And so on.

These 8 intervals in the major scale fall into one of two qualities, *perfect or major.*

Let's begin with the perfect intervals.

Perfect Intervals

There are 4 perfect intervals in a major scale. 1st, 4th, 5th, and 8th (however, the *1st and 8th* are never called that).

A *Perfect 1st* is called a **Perfect Unison,** and a *Perfect 8th* is called a **Perfect Octave.**

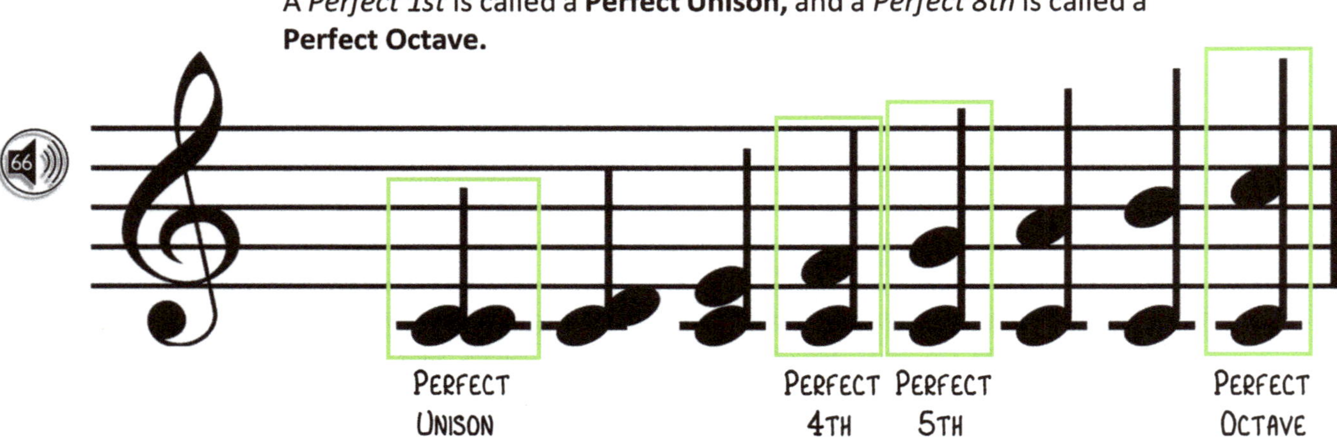

These 4 intervals are considered "perfect" because they were traditionally considered "perfectly consonant", or pleasant, as opposed to being dissonant (or crunchy sounding).

But how do you know these are the intervals you're playing?

Well, eventually you'll probably just know. But for now, you can count *half-steps and whole-steps* to make sure you have the right intervals.

Perfect Unison = 0 half-steps and whole-steps
Perfect 4th = 2 whole-steps and 1 half-step, or **2.5 steps** (*W W H*)
Perfect 5th = 3 whole-steps and 1 half-step, or **3.5 steps** (*W W H W*)
Perfect Octave = 6 whole-steps (*W W H W W W H*) [2 "H" = 1 "W"]

I simplified things a bit with the half-step/whole-step game. Thinking of whole-steps as whole numbers and half-steps as the half numbers will streamline things for you.

Major Intervals

That leaves us with the remaining 4 intervals, which are major: the 2nd, 3rd, 6th, and 7th.

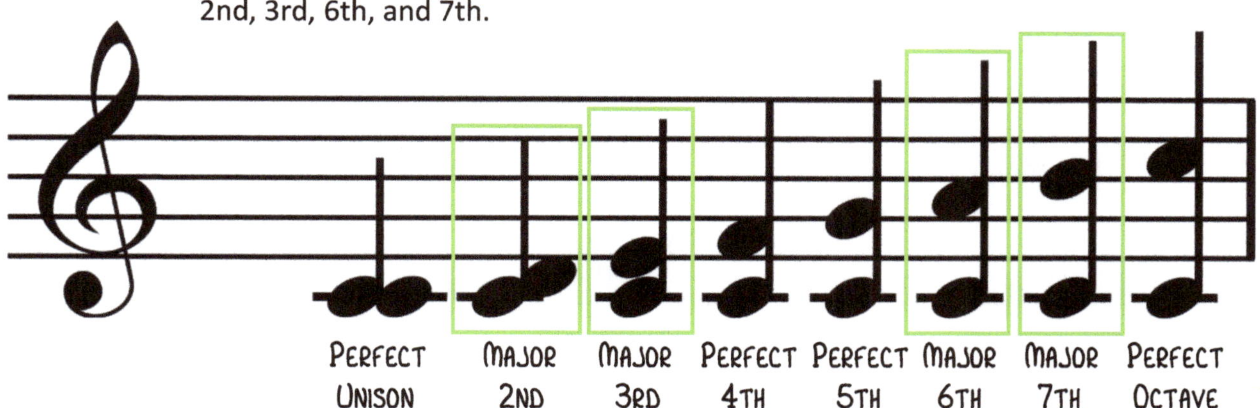

Major 2nd = 1 step (*W*)
Major 3rd = 2 steps (*W W*)
Major 6th = 4.5 steps (*W W H W W*)
Major 7th = 5.5 steps (*W W H W W W*)

That's quite a lot to write each time you need to spell one of these out. So, let's simplify these a bit. We'll use a capitol "**P**" for "Perfect" and a capitol "**M**" for "Major". And, unfortunately (or fortunately?), for this system to work we need to go back to our "**1**" for the *unison* and "**8**" for the *octave*.

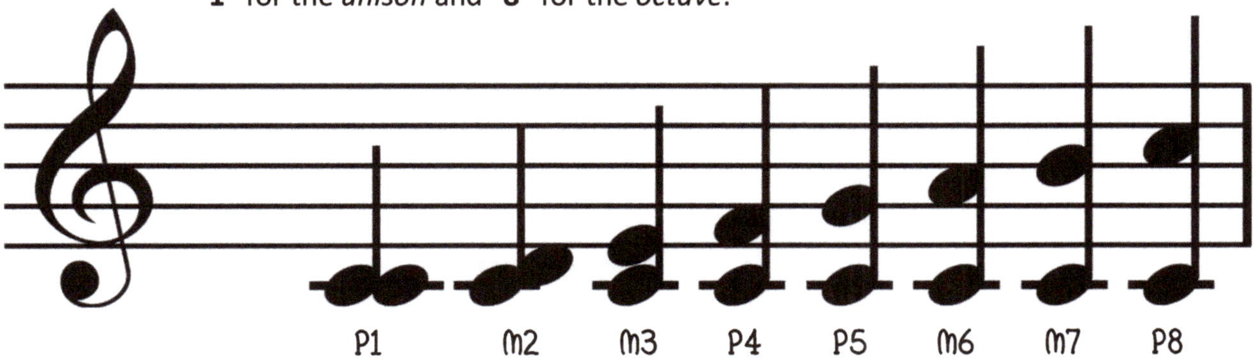

That's it - Perfect and Major intervals are set!

Minor Intervals

Minor intervals are created by shrinking a major interval by a half-step. So, they can only occur on the major intervals: 2nd, 3rd, 6th, or 7th. Also, let's jump right to the shortened version of "Minor": "m̄". This is a lowercase "m" with a bar over it. You will see many variations on this. I find this one to be the clearest. I'll put the major and minor intervals next to each other to show the difference.

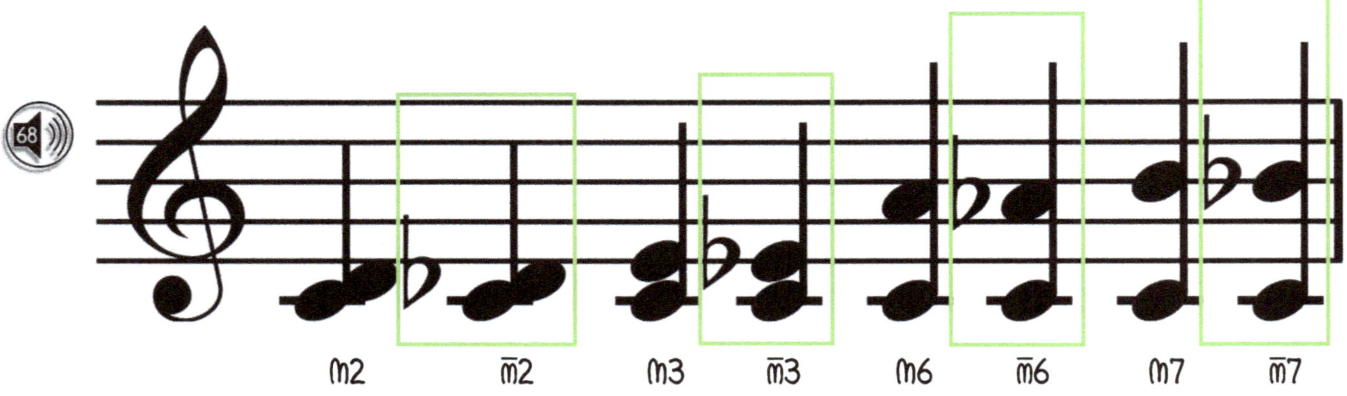

m̄2 = 1 half-step
m̄3 = 1.5 steps
m̄6 = 4 steps
m̄7 = 5 steps

Diminished and Augmented Intervals

We altered the major intervals and turned them into minor intervals. Now it's time to alter the perfect intervals.

There are two ways to alter a perfect interval with half-steps: *decrease* or *increase* its size. If you decrease its size, it becomes **diminished.** If you increase its size, it becomes **augmented.**

Makes sense, right?

> *Quick Note!* __Decreasing__ __Perfect__ __Intervals__
>
> When you decrease the size of a major interval it becomes minor. A perfect interval is never considered minor. A decreased perfect interval becomes diminished.

There are a number of reasons to call intervals by different names (usually having to do with spelling specific chords or scales). You could call a m̄2 an "Augmented 1" if you had to, but it's not common. So, I'm just going to go over the common diminished and augmented intervals you're likely to see.

Also, we're going to go with a "**+**" for "Augmented", and " **°** " for "diminished". You'll see people use other abbreviations for these, but these are the most common.

I'll add the P4 and P5 as reference.

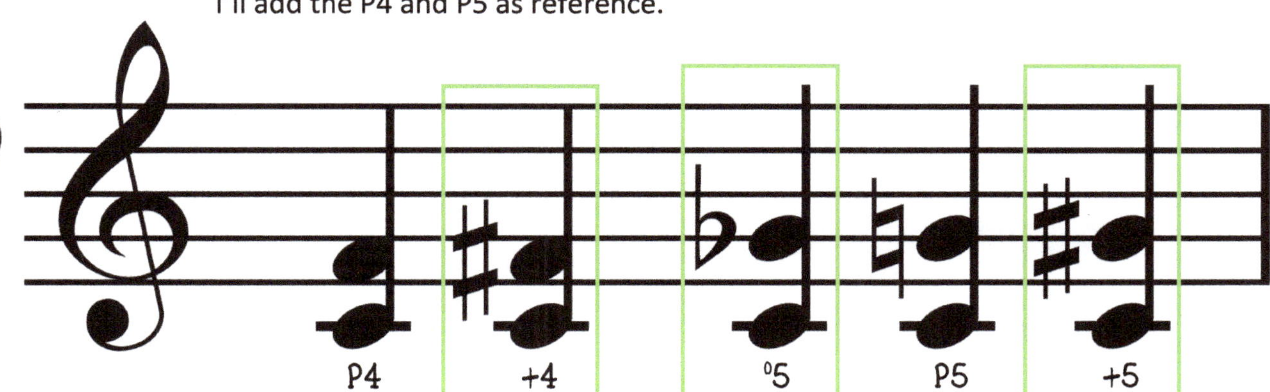

___

***Quick Note!* <u>The Devil's Interval</u>**

The +4 and °5 are the *same interval*: the **Tritone**. In early music it was considered to have an "evil" sound to it. Hard to blame them... it is pretty dissonant.

In contemporary music, the tritone serves an important role in giving music forward momentum. The 2 notes used in a tritone often push the listener's ear toward a musical resolution. This interval also happens to cut the octave exactly in half.

___

More Diminished/Augmented Talk

There are times when you need a minor interval to be smaller and a major interval to be larger. A *minor interval* which is a *half-step smaller* is also called **diminished**. And a *major interval* a *half-step larger* is also called **augmented**. You'll run into the *Diminished 7th* most often.

Now let's lay these intervals out so you can really see how they're related.

STEPS	INTERVAL	ABBREVIATION
0	Perfect Unison	P1
1 half-step	Minor 2nd	$\overline{m}2$
1 step	Major 2nd	M2
1.5 steps	Minor 3rd	$\overline{m}3$
2 steps	Major 3rd	M3
2.5 steps	Perfect 4th	P4
3 steps	Augmented 4th	+4
	Diminished 5th	°5
	(*Tritone*)	
3.5 steps	Perfect 5th	P5
4 steps	Augmented 5th	+5
	Minor 6th	$\overline{m}6$
4.5 steps	Major 6th	M6
	Diminished 7th	°7
5 steps	Minor 7th	$\overline{m}7$
5.5 steps	Major 7th	M7
6 steps	Perfect Octave	P8

COMPOUND INTERVALS

You didn't think that was it, did you? There's always something to further complicate things. The intervals above are considered **Simple Intervals**. Simple intervals are intervals *within a single octave*. **Compound Intervals** are then intervals which go *beyond a single octave*. But they're not as scary as they sound.

We've looked at the simple intervals:

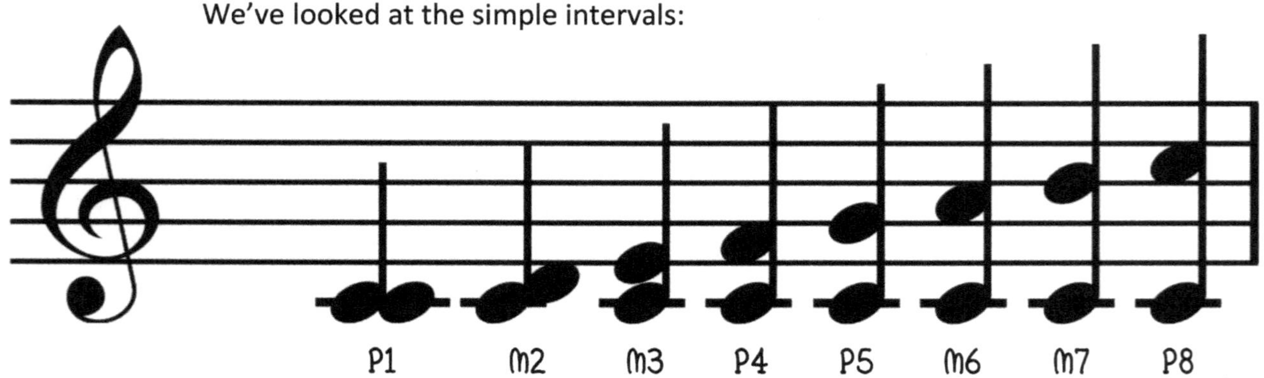

Now let's start at the octave and continue expanding.

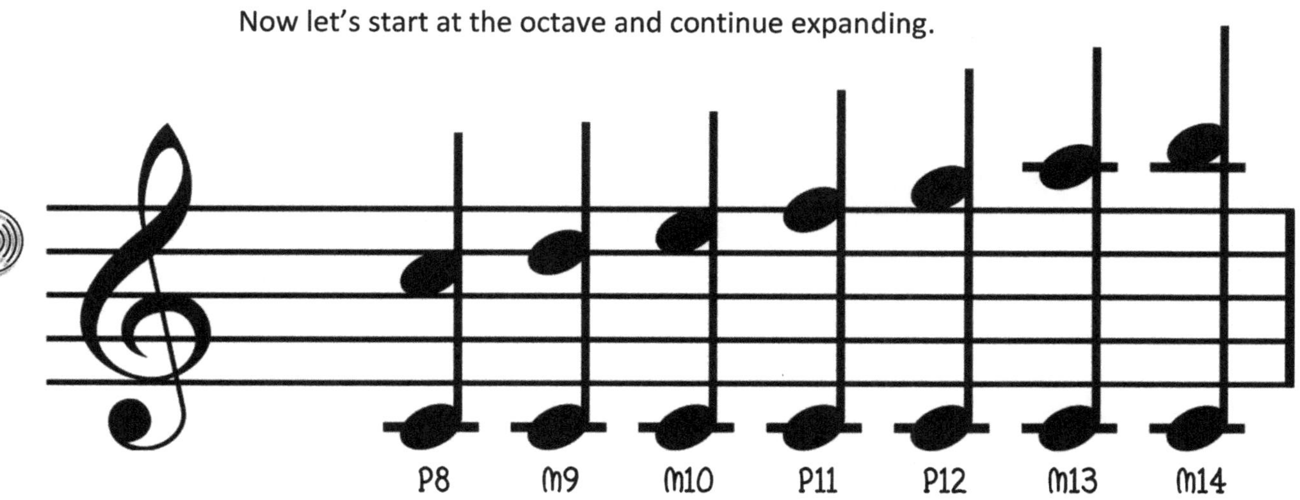

The numbers just keep going up. And if you take the "P8" off the staff with the simple intervals, do you notice anything?

The qualities of the intervals match up!

P1 and P8, M2 and M9, M3 and M10, etc.

In our example where we use the C Major Scale:

C to C = P1 and P8
C to D = M2 and M9
C to E = M3 and M10

And so on.

The compound intervals are just the *simple intervals plus 7* (the number of notes that make up a single octave). So, though there are numbers above 7 (8, 9, 10…), they're really just equivalents of our lower numbers (1, 2, 3…).

So:

P1 + 7 = P8
M2 + 7 = M9
M3 + 7 = M10

And!
The same quality rules (P, M, m̄, +, and °) of the simple intervals apply to the qualities of the compound intervals.

And even better!
You'll generally encounter only 3 of these: 9, 11, 13.

But you'll find them in many different qualities:

m̄9, M9, P11, +11, m̄13, and M13 are the most likely.

But why only these 3 compound intervals?

The 1, 3, 5, and 7 - which would translate as the 8, 10, 12, and 14 - are pretty important basic chord tones and tend to be labeled as 1, 3, 5, and 7. No sense in confusing people with these.

2, 4, and 6 turn into 9, 11, and 13. These are commonly used as *chord extensions* which add color to the basic chords.

THE CRASH

-There are two ways to think of **Intervals**
>**Harmonic** (*vertical*)
>*And*
>**Melodic** (*horizontal*)

-There are 5 core interval qualities
>**Perfect (P), Major (M), Minor (m̄), Augmented (+),** and **Diminished (°)**

-**Major Intervals** decrease by a half-step to become **Minor Intervals**

-**Perfect Intervals: decrease** to become **Diminished Intervals**
>**increase** to become **Augmented Intervals**

-Occasionally, you'll: **decrease** a **Minor** to become **Diminished**, or
>**increase** a **Major** to become **Augmented**

-**Perfect Intervals = P1, P4, P5, P8**
-**Major Intervals = M2, M3, M6, M7**
-**Minor Intervals = m̄2, m̄3, m̄6, m̄7**
-**Augmented Intervals = +4, +5**
-**Diminished Intervals = °5, °7**

-**Compound Intervals** go beyond a single octave
>-They are the **Simple Intervals + 7**
>-**9, 11,** and **13** are the most common

Okay, let's get away from the notes a bit and back to the staff!

CHAPTER 12
EVEN MORE STAFF

So far, we've learned about the *lines and spaces*, *bar lines*, some important *clefs*, and *the grand staff*. Let's dig into some other fundamental things you should know.

KEY SIGNATURES

While it's absolutely possible to just use accidentals (*sharps, flats, and naturals*) to compose a piece of music in any key, it could get tedious to read.

This is where **Key Signatures** come in.

Keys signatures help alleviate the need for too many accidentals by telling you which notes should always be flat or sharp (or occasionally natural) right at the beginning of the staff.

By telling you which notes should be flat, sharp, or natural, they also tell you which **Key** the song is in, or which note is **"1"**.

The key signature above has *6 flats* and is the key signature for Gb Major. Gb is *"1"*. We'll get into how you'll know that's Gb Major in just a bit.

For now, just know that once you figure out which note is "1" you can build the scale using our formulas from "Chapter 6".

Major Scale = **WWH WWWH**
Minor Scale = **WH WWH WW**

G♭ Major Scale = G♭ A♭ B♭ C♭ D♭ E♭ F G♭

(Notice our enharmonic spelling of *B Natural* as the C♭. You can't have 2 of the same letter in a major scale.)

The key signature then helps this mess:

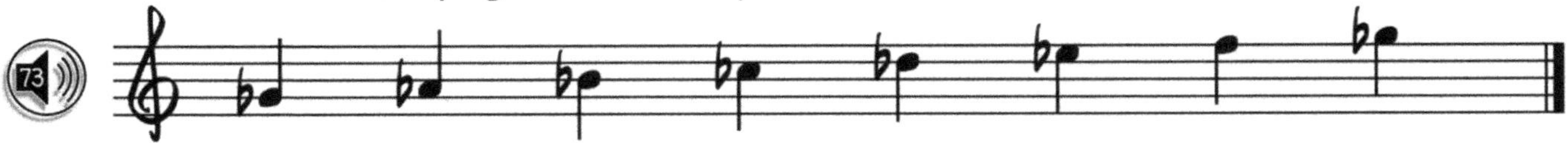

To become this:

THE CIRCLE OF FIFTHS

You could just memorize which key signature goes with which key (and you eventually will!). But there are also helpful ways of quickly figuring this out. One of the most helpful tools for this is the **Circle of Fifths.**

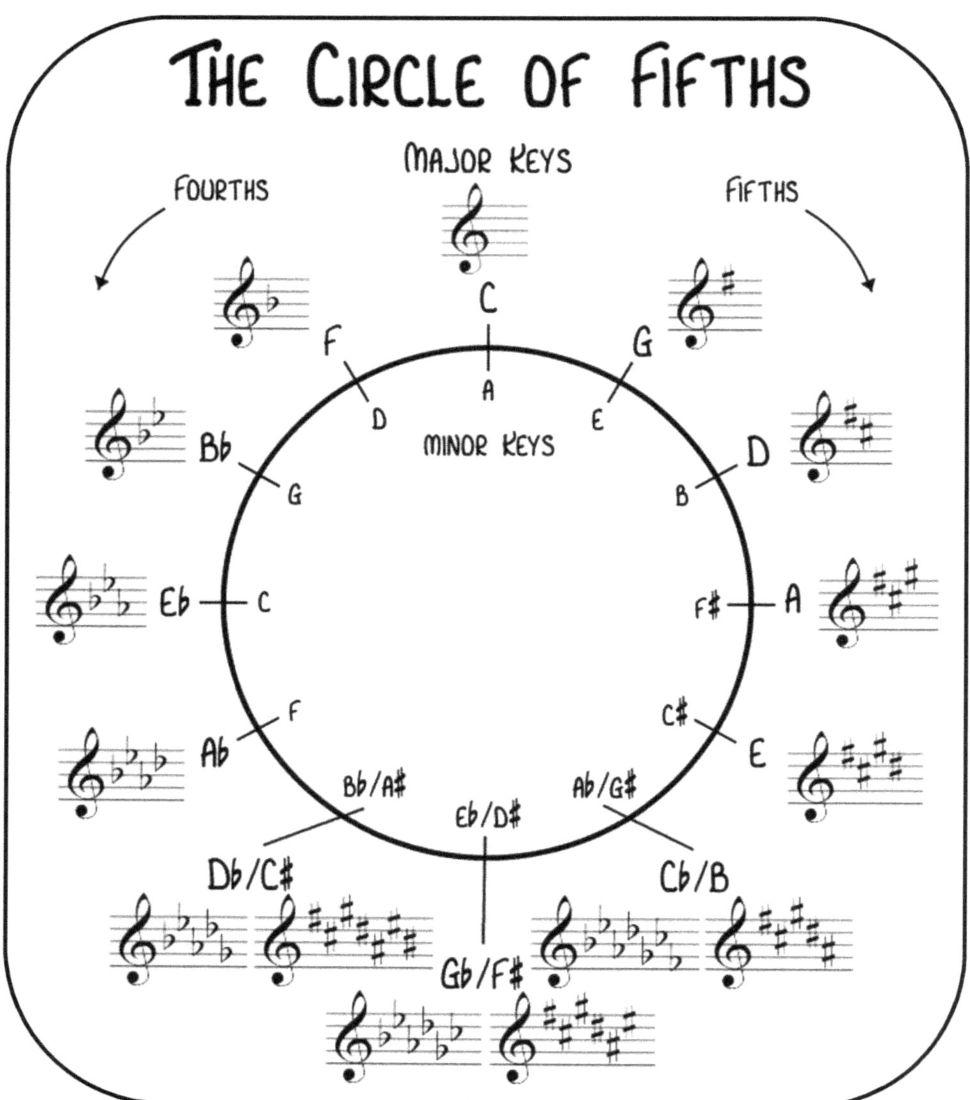

The Circle of Fifths could just as easily have been called "The Circle of Fourths"... but it wasn't. The version you see here is a simple version of the circle for our purposes, but if you really dive into it, the circle can give you some serious insight into musical theory.

Dissecting The Circle of Fifths

Let me explain what you're looking at. If you remember our intervals, this will all make a lot more sense.

-Moving *clockwise* around the circle we go *up by fifths*. Moving *counterclockwise* we go *up by fourths*. Both sides are important to understanding key signatures.

-On the outside of the circle are the names of the *Major Keys* and the key signatures that go with them.

-On the inside of the circle are the *relative Minor Keys* to those Major Keys.

What?! I only have to remember one key signature for both the Major Keys and their relative Minor Keys??

That's right! Remember that the relative minor key starts on the *6th scale degree* of the major key. In the key of C Major, the relative minor key is A Minor. They both use the *same notes* and *key signature*, they just start on a different *first note* (in music-speak, a different *tonic*).

-On the bottom of the circle, there are 3 slots that each have 2 letters and 2 key signatures associated with them. If we recall our enharmonic spellings, D♭ and C♯ are the same note, G♭ and F♯ are the same note, and C♭ and B are the same note. Generally, you'll use the key signature with fewer accidentals... D♭ instead of C♯, and B instead of C♭... but not always. And G♭ and F♯ have the same number of accidentals, so, up to you!

How This Is Helpful

The key of C Major is always a good starting point. C Major has no flats or sharps in its key signature. Phew. If you then move clockwise through the fifths, each key has *1 more sharp* in the key signature. G has 1 sharp, D has 2 sharps, and so on. Moving the other way, counterclockwise, through the fourths, each key has *1 more flat* in the key signature. F has 1 flat, B♭ has 2 flats, etc.

So, we need to memorize the fourths and the fifths.

Here's my recommendation: let's flatten the circle into 2 lines. The order will make sense in a minute.

Line of Fourths (*order of flats*) = **B E A D G C F B♭ E♭ A♭ D♭ G♭**

Line of Fifths (*order of sharps*) = **F C G D A E B**

Recite these 2 lines every night before you turn out the lights.

When put together they cover all the key signatures in the circle. But even more importantly, they tell you the *order of the flats and sharps in the key signatures*!

Flat Keys

F Major = 1 flat = the flat is on "B"

Now let's move all the way to the bottom of the "Fourths" side to the key of:

C♭ Major = 7 flats = the flats are on "B", "E", "A", "D", "G", "C", "F".

Did those flats look familiar? They come straight from the "Line of Fourths"!

Sharp Keys

G Major = 1 sharp = the sharp is on the "F".
I bet you can see where this is headed.

Move all the way to the bottom of the "Fifths" side to:

C♯ Major = 7 sharps = "F", "C", "G", "D", "A", "E", "B".

Straight from the "Line of Fifths"!

Now I know how to add sharps and flats to a staff to CREATE the key signatures, but how do I just read the key signatures?

There are a couple tricks to learn for that until you can just look at them and know.

Flat Key Signatures

The trick with flat key signatures is to look at the **second to last flat**.

Let's take the key signature with 2 flats. As we've learned, they are on "B" and "E".

The *second to last flat* is **B♭.**

This is the key signature for the key of **B♭ Major.**

Let's try another one.

Let's do the key signature with 4 flats. We know they're on "B", "E", "A", and "D".

The *second to last flat* is **A♭.**

This is the key signature for the key of **A♭ Major.**

With flat key signatures, the *second to last flat* is the key you're in. This is *almost* a perfect system.

This method breaks down with the key of **F Major**, because:

F Major only has **1 flat**.

There is no "second to last" flat to look for.
So, you just have to memorize this one.

Sharp Key Signatures

This trick doesn't have any exceptions to throw you off.
For sharp key signatures you **find the last sharp, and go up a half-step**.

Let's start with 1 sharp. We know that goes on the "F".

A *half-step up* from F♯ is G.

This is **G Major.**

What about 3 sharps? We know they're on "F", "C", and "G".

A *half-step up* from G♯ is A.

This is **A Major.**

THE CRASH

-**Key Signatures** tell you which key you're in and which notes should be flat or sharp

-**The Circle of Fifths** is a handy tool when it comes to key signatures

- **Line of Fourths** (*order of flats*) = **B E A D G C F B♭ E♭ A♭ D♭ G♭**

-**Line of Fifths** (*order of sharps*) = **F C G D A E B**

Tricks For Naming the Key:
-If the key signature has **flats**, the **second to last flat** is the key
-If you're looking at **sharps**, a **half-step up from the last sharp** is the key

-C Major has no flats or sharps

-You just have to memorize that **F Major** has **1 flat**

FINAL WORDS

That was probably a lot of info if you're new to music theory. And if you're not new, I hope it was a good refresher. It's a lifelong journey to fully demystify contemporary music theory (or any other aspect of music theory for that matter). Every time you think you're getting a handle on some aspect you find five new questions to dive headlong into.

This book is just a jumping off point. It gave you the basics of what you're looking at on the staff, rhythm and counting, where the notes go and how they can be altered, how basic scales and intervals are constructed, and how to know which key you're in. You probably have *at least* five new questions for each of these ideas. That's great! Ask those questions and seek those answers!

Everybody starts learning music theory at the beginning. Nobody just *knows* this stuff. While it doesn't take much work to get a basic understanding of what you're looking at, it will take time and practice to really learn music theory. I still remember my first week of music school when I learned what a tritone is - the concept blew me away! Now it seems like just another music theory fundamental.

I hope this book helped to light a music theory learning fire under you and you keep moving forward. Music theory - and music!! - just get richer and more exciting the further you go. So, get out there and keep music-ing!

-Jeff

FINAL FINAL WORDS

Please consider leaving a review of this book. I would greatly appreciate it. It will help me to continue on this book writing journey, as this series is ultimately planned to have 3 books in it.

Thank you in advance!

LEAVE A REVIEW

(https://amzn.to/47jfPs2)

HARMONYTABS EMAIL LIST

Once again, here is the link to the HarmonyTabs email list to keep you up to speed on any new music, publications, and promotions.

(https://www.harmonytabs.com/email-list/)

ACKNOWLEDGEMENTS

First and foremost, I need to thank my son Ollie. Without his birth, I would never have found myself stuck quietly on the couch late at night. Those couple hours each night is the time I found to devote to this book.

Next is his patient mother Kristen; my partner and a key editor. She sat through my thought process during many of Ollie's meals and helped me restructure my phrasing so I sound less like a troglodyte.

And my remaining editors… but friends first. Dan, who sifted through this book to correct even the most minor detail, and made critical edits on nearly every page – and who really tried to get me to place the punctuation marks inside many of the quotation marks… but I simply refuse; Peter, whose insights will hopefully draw more traffic to this book; Alisha, who pointed out a few key things which obviously needed to be changed once I saw them; and Chris, who once again helped me clear up issues that would have undoubtedly led to confusion.

Thank you all so much!

ABOUT THE AUTHOR

Jeff Bratz has a degree in Professional Music from the School for Music Vocations and a Professional Certificate in Music Theory and Composition from Berklee College of Music. He's a composer and arranger specializing in vocal arrangements. In a former life, Jeff was a music teacher for grades pre-k through high school. He has sung in dozens of vocal groups including The Dickens Carolers at Disneyland's *Club 33*, The Fault Line on *America's Got Talent*, and Manhattan Transfer tribute group LA Transfer. He was also part of the Downbeat award-winning First Take. He currently performs with rock band RaDIUM, 80s rock tribute band 8IGHTY 6IXX, and salsa band Calle Mambo. He lives in Pasadena with his wonderful partner Kristen and the cutest nugget that ever nuggeted: Ollie!

Also Available From

HarmonyTabs

Sheet Music

-A Cappella Choirs/Groups
-Brass Ensembles
-String Ensembles
-Sax Ensembles
And More!

HARMONYTABS.COM/SHEET-MUSIC/

Songbooks

-Wind Ensembles
-A Cappella Choirs/Groups
-Flute Ensembles
-Brass Ensembles
And More!

HARMONYTABS.COM/MUSIC-BOOKS/SONGBOOKS/

Music Theory and Instruction

-An Incomplete Crash Course
in Contemporary Music Theory:
The Fundamentals

More to Come!

HARMONYTABS.COM/MUSIC-BOOKS/INSTRUCTIONAL-BOOKS/

Music Composition

-Standard Manuscript Notebook
-Pocket Manuscript Notebook
-Writing Prompt Journals

More to Come!

HARMONYTABS.COM/MUSIC-BOOKS/MUSIC-COMPOSITION-BOOKS/

HarmonyTabsMusic.com

www.ingramcontent.com/pod-product-compliance
Lightning Source LLC
Chambersburg PA
CBHW041034050726
47599CB00018B/1958